Advance Praise for *The Re*

"Family enterprises thrive on long-term vision, strong values, and commitment to their people and communities. In his book, *The Retention Trap*, Mark Peters insightfully reframes conventional thinking around talent investment and the talent system in a way that most family business leaders will find compelling. *The Retention Trap* is an essential read for those who want to create a legacy by developing people, not just retaining them."

—Greg McCann, Founder and Senior Advisor, Generation6

"Mark Peters presents a transformative approach to workforce management that is timely and essential. *The Retention Trap* challenges outdated notions of employee retention and offers a forward-thinking framework for investing in talent as a strategic asset. Drawing on real-world experience and compelling case studies, Peters makes a persuasive case for why businesses must move beyond retention metrics and embrace a more holistic, human-centered approach to talent development. This book is a must-read for leaders navigating the evolving world of work."

—Joseph Fuller, Professor of Management
Practice & Co-Founder of Managing the Future
of Work, Harvard Business School

"In *The Retention Trap*, Mark Peters delivers a powerful call to action for leaders in healthcare and beyond. He challenges conventional retention strategies and offers a visionary approach to investing in talent—one that fosters growth, engagement, and long-term success. In an industry where workforce stability is critical to patient care and operational excellence, this book provides invaluable insights for building a resilient and motivated workforce. A must-read for healthcare executives and HR leaders alike."

—Kevin Vos, Senior Vice President of Facilities
and Support Services, Corewell Health

"As a business owner, I know firsthand the challenges of attracting and keeping top talent. *The Retention Trap* is a game-changer—Mark Peters dismantles outdated retention strategies and offers a forward-thinking approach that prioritizes talent investment and long-term business success. His insights are practical, actionable, and essential for any leader looking to build a resilient and engaged workforce in today's competitive market."

—Mike Betts, Chairman and CEO, Betts Company

"Mark Peters presents a compelling and well-researched argument for rethinking workforce economics in *The Retention Trap*. In a time where our demographic profile argues for a worsening labor shortage, he challenges leaders to embrace talent investment and their own role in the talent system as a key driver of productivity, innovation, and economic resilience. His insights bridge the gap between business strategy and labor market realities, making this book essential reading for economists, policymakers, and business leaders alike."

—Jeffrey Korzenik, economist and author of *Untapped Talent*

"Mark Peters delivers a groundbreaking approach to workforce strategy in *The Retention Trap*—one that manufacturing leaders cannot afford to ignore. In an industry where skilled labor shortages and high turnover present ongoing challenges, Peters offers a compelling case for shifting from reactive retention tactics to proactive talent investment. His insights provide a roadmap for manufacturers looking to build a more engaged, skilled, and future-ready workforce. A must-read for industry leaders committed to long-term success."

—Genelle Taylor Kumpe, CEO, San Joaquin Valley Manufacturing Alliance and Fresno Business Council

THE
RETENTION
TRAP

THE RETENTION TRAP

STOP MEASURING TURNOVER, START MEASURING TALENT INVESTMENT

MARK PETERS

A POST HILL PRESS BOOK
ISBN: 979-8-88845-621-7
ISBN (eBook): 979-8-88845-622-4

The Retention Trap:
Stop Measuring Turnover, Start Measuring Talent Investment
© 2025 by Mark Peters
All Rights Reserved

Cover design by Jim Villaflores
Cover concept by The Ink Factory

This book, as well as any other Post Hill Press publications, may be purchased in bulk quantities at a special discounted rate. Contact orders@posthillpress.com for more information.

This is a work of nonfiction. All people, locations, events, and situations are portrayed to the best of the author's memory.

No part of this book may be reproduced, stored in a retrieval system, or transmitted by any means without the written permission of the author and publisher.

Post Hill Press
New York • Nashville
posthillpress.com

Published in the United States of America
1 2 3 4 5 6 7 8 9 10

To my parents, who are no longer living: To my mother, with whom I shared a deep and heartfelt connection—your love and understanding have always been my guiding light. And to my father, whose tough expectations pushed me to grow in ways I couldn't have imagined. Though our relationship was challenging, I now recognize the strength and resilience you instilled in me, lessons that have shaped who I am today.

To all the remarkable individuals who started with me in entry-level roles and seized the opportunities and support we provided. Through your perseverance and the tough choices you made day after day, you transformed your lives—and the lives of your families. I am deeply grateful for the commitment and engagement you brought back to the business, which not only fueled our success but also inspires me every day to continue this important and life-changing work.

To Carrie Link, my executive assistant and life integrator: Your tireless enthusiasm, curiosity, and dedication have been the driving force behind bringing this book to life. I am deeply grateful for your unwavering support and the countless ways you've helped me stay focused and organized. To my entire executive team and the members of my Vistage group: Your insights, guidance, and shared wisdom have been invaluable throughout this journey. Your commitment and collaboration have not only contributed to this book but have also been instrumental in the success and growth of our business.

And finally, to my daughter, Isabella, as you embark on your journey to college. I love you dearly, and when you open this book, I hope you'll recognize the passion and dedication I've poured into my work—something I hope you've glimpsed during our many conversations at the kitchen table. My greatest wish for you is that you discover your own passions and pursue them with the same intensity and love that has driven me.

CONTENTS

Foreword xi
Introduction xiii

Part One: Setting Out

Chapter One: Our Talent System Is Broken 3
Chapter Two: My Early Introduction to the World
    and Its Schisms 16
Chapter Three: Empathy in an Enterprise 25
Chapter Four: Building The SOURCE 33
Chapter Five: The Key to Thriving in These
    Fast-Changing Times Is Being Talent-Centric,
    Not Enterprise-Centric 40
Chapter Six: What We Need to Understand about
    the Rate of Change and the Future of Work 46

Part Two: Seeing Ahead

Chapter Seven: New Ways Big Companies Are
    Thinking About Talent 61
Chapter Eight: What We Get to Do as Small- and
    Medium-Sized-Business Leaders 71

Part Three: Today's Visionary Leaders

Chapter Nine: Standing on the Shoulders of Giants.............81
Chapter Ten: Pioneers on the Path 90
Chapter Eleven: Little Things Can Have a Big Impact........102
Chapter Twelve: A Way Out and Up 111
Chapter Thirteen: Learning from the Swiss 118
Chapter Fourteen: The Talent Pipeline 127
Chapter Fifteen: R.I.S.E. Up 139

Part Four: Succeeding

Chapter Sixteen: Redefining Success...................................147
Chapter Seventeen: The Integration 150
Chapter Eighteen: How Systems Thinking Can
    Help Us Create Better Talent Flow...............................154
Chapter Nineteen: Dragons at the Threshold 178
Chapter Twenty: Planting Seeds of Change 186

Conclusion...195
Resources 199
Acknowledgments 201
About the Author..203

FOREWORD

When Mark asked me to write the forward to his second book, I was honored. After reading it, I am inspired and grateful. He speaks business, entrepreneurship, and human development fluently because he lives them. He can reach the people with the talent, influence, and resources to help solve intractable issues and restore confidence. He can reach people who are struggling because he cares. He explains how business leaders can help integrate human and economic development within their enterprises, with peers in their community, and politically across sectors. Enough do this and we will create the environments and systems all residents need to achieve their potential and our economies to thrive.

The Retention Trap aligns with advances in science. More people are realizing quantum physics is the practical application of ancient wisdom. We are all connected, interdependent. Our founders knew this. E pluribus unum—out of many, one—is on the Great Seal of the United States and our currency. The American dream exists as a possibility. To manifest it requires us to become the people we are called to be and do our part. All matter. Much like a jigsaw puzzle, there are no extra pieces, and we are not done until everyone plays. But first, we must turn our piece over, so we know where we fit. We all have a unique role to play. Mark's book challenges us to do this. As he explains, it is in our personal and collective self-interest to do so.

As he points out, one of the challenges is personal, the inner work. Are enough of us willing to release the unresolved trauma and social conditioning we absorb as children and open our minds? What if the pursuit of happiness is not just material but must include the path to integrity? Martin Luther King, Jr. saw this. He envisioned a time when we would be judged not by the details that can divide us, but our character and contributions.

When we stopped teaching civics decades ago, the compounding impact of this failure led to a dangerous wealth gap and loss of faith in one another, our institutions and our future. Mark's book offers practical guidelines and a compass to renew the dream, clarify essential roles, and invite the three sectors to integrate their efforts to advance the common good. Together, we can create inclusive prosperity and wellbeing.

I feel his urgency. I believe in the path because I live in a city—Fresno, California—that is on its way. We have amazing leaders across sectors with the courage to risk social, financial, and political capital to invest in the American dream and liberate the human spirit.

Deborah Nankivell

Deborah is CEO of the Fresno Stewardship Foundation and before that roll was CEO of the Fresno Business Council for thirty years, building where she shepherded the business civic groups combined skill and resource to improve critical aspect of the community and region. She was also instrumental in starting Heartland Compass, an adaptation of The SOURCE, serving Fresno businesses. She has published two books: *Civic Stewardship* and *Bugle Call*.

INTRODUCTION

When I was twelve, my father, a tough Midwestern businessman and inventor, told me my free-wheeling summers were over. It was time to work in the yard or Butterball Farms, Inc., my dad's factory. I chose the yard, of course. But within three days, my allergies forced me to change course. I ended up in Dad's food plant's temperature-controlled, filtered-air environment.

On my first day, he gathered the supervisors around his desk and introduced me. He told them even though I was his son, if I did anything wrong, they should just fire me. This seems strange and unlikely as an adult, but it left quite an impression on a twelve-year-old who grew up with a father who never bluffed. So, I worked hard and made a lot of friends because I was pretty sure, at some point, I was going to screw something up and need their help not to get fired.

It was also the beginning of a lifetime of learning that these friends of mine, the people who went to work every day, lived very different lives than I did. I heard them talk about choosing between buying groceries or new clothes for their kids. I learned that when their car broke down, sometimes they didn't have a few hundred dollars to fix it—which set off another set of problems because they couldn't get to work. Most of them were tired and stressed and barely getting by.

This didn't sit right with me and set me up for a life of working to reconcile how compassion and capitalism can coexist. Or, to put it in more current terms: how can capitalism be rooted in purpose and profit in these fast-changing, uncertain times? Or, to the point of this book: how can we escape the retention trap, in which employers try the same old stale tactics to get people to stay—while employees often feel like they are spinning their wheels and failing to progress, let alone get by?

I should be clear at the outset: I'm not a do-gooder. I'm a pragmatist, a problem-solver, and a businessman. And my interest in integrating value creation and purpose, which is shared by a growing number of leaders, is not merely a nice-to-have passion. At a time of so many significant problems in business, our nation, and the world—from talent shortages, to growing economic inequality, to a search for a greater sense of purpose among leaders and the people who work for them—achieving a balance between financial success and a greater sense of purpose is more than the right thing to do. It's the smart thing to do. Given some significant trends I will discuss in this book, I also believe it is essential to the survival of small and medium-sized businesses. It is an exciting thing we get to do as enterprise leaders, by defining success and value more broadly.

In this book, I argue that today's talent system is broken. Here's what I mean. Most leaders of small and mid-sized companies have been taught to carefully track their employee retention rates as an essential indicator of business strength, employee satisfaction, and management quality. Yet this traditional management metric is failing both American businesses and their workers.

After all, countless businesses still struggle with attracting and retaining talent, even though many business leaders have responded by employing the only levers believed to support retention: better pay or benefits. That's the trap. Can't get people to stay? We think: get a new staffing firm, raise wages, offer more flextime, reduce the attendance requirement, get a fitness center, put in a coffee bar, bring in new plants, provide more team-spirit shirts, find out what others in our ecosphere offer and match or exceed that.

Like our customers, our people rarely tell us what they want. But they are great at telling us what they think they need: more money! Despite the importance of living wages, statistics say money is *not* the most significant reason people stay or leave jobs. People want to feel respected, have a sense of purpose, and have development opportunities—and we have the opportunity to provide that.

In other words, retention is no longer tied to the traditional inputs Economics 101 might have us believe. We need to think differently. Some of the country's largest employers have already figured this out. Most small and mid-sized firms have not, and they are in danger of being stuck in the retention trap forever and a reinforcing loop of ever-increasing wage and benefit costs.

So, going forward, how should leaders of small and mid-sized firms think about retention, as a management metric and strategic goal? In this book, I challenge the conventional wisdom about retention rates and offer a host of new ideas and possibilities. Some have already been adopted by the nation's largest companies, and they can and must be adopted by small and mid-sized firms—the very heart of American entrepreneurship—if we are not to be left behind in tomorrow's race for talent.

In brief, I argue that we need to rethink talent, focusing on investment rather than retention. Ultimately, we need to be both talent-centric and enterprise-centric. I also argue that we need to expand the idea of value so it is tied not only to money but also to growth and purpose.

From a meta-perspective, we all know we have big problems. Many people say capitalism itself is broken. However, as my friend Geoffrey Jones of Harvard University has said, the only way to improve any system is one person, one community at a time.

As enterprise leaders, we have the opportunity to do that—for the people who work for us, for ourselves, and for the betterment of the system as a whole. Business leaders are among the best problem-solvers there are. Isn't that what we do, after all? See a problem and come up with solutions people will pay for.

Of course, very few, if any of us, get into business because we want to solve talent problems. We don't wake up one day and say, "You know, I want to hire a bunch of people, help them develop their skills, and then figure out how to make money from it."

It goes more like this: We see a problem in the marketplace that we know how to solve—or feel confident we can figure out. Then, we hire people to help us do it. Hiring and developing talent, in other words, comes as a byproduct of our primary goal, which is to build a profitable business by solving problems in the marketplace.

So, surely, we can apply these skills to the talent system—and be problem-solvers.

About Me

At this point, I should assure you this isn't just a pie-in-the-sky idea from some guy you may never have heard of. It builds on twenty years of success in a collaborative project focused on supporting talent. It is supported by many other leaders nationwide, with whom I have spoken recently, and who also recognize the need for a new approach to impacting people in our talent system.

When my father died in 1995, I took over Butterball Farms, Inc., a specialty butter company, radically changing its culture and bottom line. We have served McDonald's, among other clients, *and* repeatedly have been named among the Best and Brightest Companies to Work For®.

More than twenty years ago, I formed The SOURCE, a network that brings together community, government, and private interests to leverage existing assets to strengthen the community's workforce. We now have twenty-five member companies covering 10,800 people. Through the support systems we have put in place, we have achieved a 90 percent retention rate for individuals employed at a SOURCE member company and receiving welfare benefits, compared to a 57 percent retention rate for people receiving welfare benefits and seeing traditional state caseworkers.

We are saving the state millions of dollars *and* keeping people employed. We also provide over 330 percent return on investment, partner with over fifty local organizations, and have saved employers over $19.8 million. You can read more about this in Chapter Four and in my first book, *The Source: Using the Power of Collaboration to Stabilize Your Workforce and Impact Your Community.*

We are now working to build on this success by spearheading a movement of owners of small and medium-sized businesses who are committed to investing in talent development, and who are collaborating to create an authentic flow from business to business within the talent system. It's exciting stuff!

How This Book Is Organized

The Retention Trap is organized in four parts.

Part One lays a foundation for the discussion of innovation later in the book. I share the story of creating The SOURCE, the western Michigan collective that many local small and mid-sized manufacturers have joined to provide social services to their combined workforces. The SOURCE has helped businesses in this region treat their employees with humanity and empathy and has helped each company's bottom line.

Part Two explains big companies' significant shift to talent investment. I share insights from leading companies such as Accenture, AT&T, Bank of America, Meta, Alphabet, IBM, Intel, JPMorgan Chase, Kaiser, PwC, Salesforce, Verizon, and Virgin Group.

Part Three presents a series of case studies and examples from various successful visionaries. These leading small or mid-sized entities have already replaced traditional notions of retention with new models and approaches. These leaders have captured some of the same ideas large companies use, but tailored to the unique needs of a smaller setting. These chapters present a rich array of ideas, solutions, approaches, and possibilities that give you a new understanding of what is possible.

Finally, Part Four offers the business leader suggestions about implementation and a broader framework for understanding their workforce, which will positively impact talent, restore joy to the workplace, and, for the leader, bring greater satisfaction. This is, after all, an invitation to a different kind of leadership.

Throughout, I will weave my personal story into the argument, facts, and case studies I offer here. I do this because this is deeply personal work for me, and I hope you will connect with it on that level. But I also do it because while adopting a more mature perspective on talent investment over talent retention can be done without parallel personal development, it can be done better with personal growth.

Why I Wrote This Book

I have spent a lot of time in peer groups over the years, and yes, I have met CEOs who are self-centered SOBs driven by monetary gain. However, most of the CEOs I have encountered are good, hard-working people who generally want what is best for their families and those around them. Most of them have never spent a lot of time thinking about how to find purpose in the operation of their enterprise. I find this sad, especially when you consider what's possible.

I want us to think big, think about the long-term, and think about what we get to do with the power of our enterprises. The current drive to retain people is a short-term goal that leads to some very dollar-driven thinking, which never pays long-term dividends to the enterprise, the people working in it, or the community in which it exists.

However, when you flip the script and start thinking about opportunity, it goes like this: "We have this great opportunity to hire people and then help them find and live into their passion." How are we going to be effective at this? How do we change the "work" we do in our enterprises from a "have to go to work every day" to a "get to go help get that (plug in your company's purpose statement) done every day"?

For me, that's the gold mine. It is human potential. It is having an enterprise through which I can flow talent and have a positive and lasting influence, and which will have a positive impact on any setting those people end up in. That sort of value cannot be accomplished with cash.

So, I hope to inspire you to think, "Wow, why haven't we entertained this way of thinking before?" Then, to begin making some changes. Ultimately, I hope to show you that doing this work is also a path to a greater sense of integration—or a deep, holistic sense of purpose—for you and others who lead or wish to lead enterprises today.

I should be clear: I don't promise a neat set of answers. That's because no one neat set of solutions will work for everyone. But I do offer my story of engaging with these challenges and championing the cause—encouraging you to shift your mindset about talent, challenge long-held assumptions around retention, and reflect on what investing in talent could mean for the strategic future of you, your people, your business, and our communities.

PART ONE
SETTING OUT

CHAPTER ONE
OUR TALENT SYSTEM IS BROKEN

What is your retention number? Or your turnover number? Every HR leader everywhere has been asked those questions. The assumption is that the higher your retention number or the lower your turnover number, the better your enterprise is. But is it?

The retention problem is almost universal in business. Whether you're in healthcare, restaurants, manufacturing, or high-paying white-collar professions doesn't matter. There's virtually no enterprise where the retention conversation hasn't been an issue. It's our common pain point.

Yet the way I see it, the focus on retention and our decisions to increase it have been driving some lousy decision-making. In particular, fear-based decision-making has us focusing on the externalities surrounding the people who work for us (pay, benefits, work environment, flexibility, and so on) but very little on the people themselves. As employers, we are too often pulling our hair out, chasing too little talent—or, at least, too little of the right talent. And employees are too often left to fend for themselves to navigate changes and the new skills and expectations they bring. In short, there is very little intentionality or design to our talent systems—and a great deal of waste.

All of this stems from a lack of intentionality around talent, a far cry from the intentionality—especially around opportunity—that we bring to other aspects of our businesses, such as sales.

For example, in terms of sales, our customers tell us they want higher quality at lower prices. They tell us that all the time! But we understand that there is much more at play than that. We know that brand protection is essential and that we must connect to customers' values when selling a product. The companies that are most successful and can command the most significant margins are the ones that do a great job of understanding what their customers are driven by. They know their customers' pain points, how their product or service addresses them, and what they can provide that no one else does.

One great book on this topic is *Blue Ocean Strategy: How to Create Uncontested Market Space and Make the Competition Irrelevant* by W. Chan Kim and Renée Mauborgne. Kim and Mauborgne describe the market universe as composed of "red oceans" and "blue oceans." As they put it:

"Red oceans are all the industries in existence today. This is the known market space....

"In the red oceans, industry boundaries are defined and accepted, and the competitive rules of the game are known. Here, companies try to outperform their rivals to grab a greater share of existing demand. As the market space gets crowded, prospects for profits and growth are reduced. Products become commodities, and cutthroat competition turns the red ocean bloody."

Blue oceans, in contrast, "denote all the industries *not* in existence today. This is the unknown market space," untainted by competition. In blue oceans, demand is created rather than fought over. There is ample opportunity for growth that is both profitable and rapid.

In blue oceans, competition is irrelevant because the rules of the game are waiting to be set. A blue ocean is an analogy for the wider, deeper potential to be found in unexplored market space. It is vast, deep, and powerful in terms of profitable growth.

Another great book that speaks to this is *Whale Hunting: How to Land Big Sales and Transform Your Company* by Tom Searcy and Barbara Weaver Smith. They use the analogy of the Inuit people of the Arctic who risk a great deal to hunt the mighty whale, even though they could catch fish and hunt caribou much more easily. Why? Because a single whale can provide a village with food and oil for a year.

"It's the same in the sales business," the authors note; "small fish will keep you fed, but landing each whale-size account can fill your corporate belly for years." They go on to argue there is a proven method for doing this.

Reading this book gave me one of my big *aha* moments around dealing with big customers. I came to understand there are very few decision-makers. For example, everyone can say no when you are in a room of five or six people. But only one can say yes. So, you need to understand their backgrounds and appeal to everyone because the goal is for no one to say no. That is the only way you can get the one to say yes.

This takes a lot of intentionality. You have to understand who is on their team and who you need to have on your team to alleviate the fears of a person who could say no. It means thinking about what's driving all the people there.

Many of us think about customers this way. But we haven't thought about talent or people that way for generations. People just come in and out of our organizations. But imagine if we looked at talent—if we *understood* talent—the same way we understand our customers. Imagine if we understood their values, pain points, and wants. How much more effective would our organizations be?

I would be surprised if any honest CEO could say that they spend 10 percent of their time thinking about what is important to the people who work for them. They may spend that time thinking about wages, benefits, and compliance. But rarely are they spending it trying to design opportunities that will be attractive to people.

Drive for retention or reducing turnover takes your eye off the ball. Worrying about what it costs you, and not why people want to stay, is a misdirection. We would be better off investing time, energy, and resources in connecting on those more profound values, pain points, and wants than on surface wage issues.

In short, our lack of intentionality around talent creates waste in the system—for both employers and employees.

Waste from the Employer's Perspective

As a manufacturer, I have always been surprised by how we can apply many resources to drive waste out of a manufacturing system—but not the talent system. We accept lean manufacturing principles, understanding that there's a cost every time there's waste or turbulence in the system. For example, we recognize waste in over and underproduction, over- and under-processing, unnecessary transportation, unnecessary motion, excess inventory, waiting, defects, and the unused creativity of team members.

But we rarely ponder what waste looks like in the talent system. And, if we ever do contemplate it, we never actually *do* anything about it.

So, what does waste look like?

There are, of course, different types of turnover: short-term (when people start and leave within ninety days), mid-term (when they do so within ninety days to eighteen months), and longer-term (when they leave after eighteen months.) For the employer, it looks like lost productivity, loss of quality products or services, more injuries, workplace disruption, absenteeism, a decline in efficiency for HR and training staff, payroll staff time spent adding and subtracting people, and required compliance work for every person coming into and leaving our enterprises.

Think about how often we bring people in without truly understanding them, and say: Here's your job, and here's what we'll pay you for it. But we don't help create their purpose-driven connection to the organization. We may succeed at out-bidding our external competitors for the particular skill set we need but not connecting the person's purpose to our own. As a result, the people working for us may not care whether we are successful. There is no "stickiness" to the relationship.

To invoke the sales analogy again, if I go to market at a discount price, I always get customers looking for deals. Similarly, if I go to market for talent by offering the next best financial deal, I end up with people not attracted to the organization because of what we do or why, but attracted only to the money. That means the next time they have the chance to get a better financial deal, they'll probably take it. And especially as a mid-market-sized business with limited career paths, I'm taking a considerable risk. I may pay a lot to get a certain kind of talent, and then risk that person leaving for the next best salary offer in six months to a year.

And just think about the cost. We calculated that every turnover event cost our business $10,000. And we had 120 turnover events last year. That's $1,200,000 in one year. That's the cost of a lack of intentionality around the talent relationship alone. On top of that, the cost of quality and production defects, equipment downturn, and injuries can be traced to not having the right talent or properly trained talent. With talent churn, we also lose out on getting creative problem-solving and the best use of talent from every person in the organization.

Waste from Our Employees' Perspective

This does not include the "system" waste experienced by the individual—that is, turnover because the job is not the right fit (skill set or interest-based), or because there is no future opportunity, or because of bad leadership (culture). For many people, there is also a wasteful ebb and flow of a dynamic like this. They think: "If I want to get to the next job, I must return to school." But getting significantly more education would place considerable demands on their time. They think: "I must quit working or work part-time to get this degree." And then they just don't do it, because they have a family and full-time jobs. Or, there aren't opportunities for advancement within the company they work for, and they just don't know where the next best job is in a community—and we think we have to hold onto them even if they want to go, and even if another employer in the community is looking for someone just like them.

In addition, it is difficult to move benefits when an employee leaves an employer. To maintain health insurance, they have to pay COBRA while waiting until they are eligible for insurance with their new employer. If they have a retirement account, they have to manage all the rollover steps. There is a lot of waste in all of that.

All this adds up to a lack of advancement opportunities, personal development opportunities, work-life balance, and to increased stress. Poverty continues to mount. And along with it, other things, like depression, substance abuse, physical abuse, loss of housing, poor health decisions, and on and on.

Now, consider more broadly our lack of intentionality in thinking about retention and talent. If we see retention as a problem, we ask the same old tired questions and try the same old tired tactics: How do we pay people more? How do we make work more flexible? How do we increase our benefits?

But we need to address what people actually need. They *say* they need more pay, different hours, and better benefits. Why? Because what we all experience in our lives creates the feeling that if we just had more money, better health insurance, or more time, things would be better.

So, we employers hope improving these things will keep our people happy—or at least on the job. Some also talk about the importance of company culture. You can go out and read many books that say, "Oh, we should treat people this way, and we should treat people that way." But it's hard for employers to be intentional about culture if they don't understand its purpose. Even I struggle with institutionalizing a better culture where our business and people will thrive, and I'm bound and determined to figure it out.

These traditional answers to retention—matching wages, hours, and benefits—keep our focus on numbers and prevent us from focusing on people. All these actions accomplish is reducing the pain our employees experience staying on the job. It's as if there are relatively few levers, but we keep pulling the same ones, even though they are not working. Yet all the statistics say people don't quit their jobs because of income. Not that that doesn't happen. It's just that they rarely list the reason as "I was underpaid." People leave jobs instead because of a lack of fulfillment, purpose, social engagement, learning, and growth. *Those* are the root cause issues.

In brief, when we are stuck in the retention trap, we get suckered into taking a limited view of value-creation. Specifically, we think the only way to provide more "value" to induce people to stay is to pay them more, increase benefits, and offer more flexibility. This is all denominated primarily in cash/money. That is the trap. Getting out requires thinking about value differently.

These are some of the ideas I will explore in this book. However, I recognize that challenging the dominant way we think about talent means suggesting a paradigm shift.

As Thomas Kuhn, one of the most influential philosophers of science of the twentieth century, famously said: "People are unlikely to jettison an unworkable paradigm, despite many indications it is not functioning properly, until a better paradigm can be presented."

A Paradigm Shift Case in Point

A paradigm, simply put, is a typical pattern or model. Very often, it is so common we take it for granted. We don't stop to question whether it's a good one. We tend to cling so firmly to patterns—of work, of life, you name it—that we may not give them up even if they are not good.

Consider one of the most significant paradigm shifts in the history of manufacturing—because if we can change paradigms in our manufacturing processes as effectively as the following story demonstrates, we can do so with our talent system.

At the end of World War II, Japan was decimated. More than 2.5 million people had died. Significant parts of Tokyo and other major cities were burned to ashes. Some 40 percent of the nation's industrial plants and infrastructure were destroyed in the war. And in total, about one-third of the nation's wealth had been wiped out.

Because the United States had a strategic interest in Japan and did not wish it to turn in its desperation to communism, it helped Japan rebuild—contributing $2.2 billion and insights from people with some new and very good ideas.

One of those people was W. Edwards Deming, a man born at the turn of the century among the first group of settlers in Powell, Wyoming. Like other pioneers at the time, Deming's family did not have an easy life. To survive, they had to be thrifty, not wasteful, and collaborate by, for example, raising barns together. These were values that would have a lifelong impact on Deming.

He went on to work his way through college at the University of Wyoming in Laramie, where he graduated with an engineering degree. He then earned a master's degree in mathematics and physics from the University of Colorado and a Ph.D. in mathematical physics from Yale University.

Turning the application of his knowledge to real-world challenges, he worked for the Department of Agriculture and published and taught mathematics and statistics. Pre-war, he served as an advisor to the US Census Bureau, where he significantly advanced survey techniques—improving accuracy and lowering costs. He taught applied statistics to engineers and others in support of the war effort.

Then, in 1947, the US Occupation authorities called him to Japan. It would be one of seven trips he would make throughout his lifetime. He taught the application of statistics to quality improvement and lectured the most prestigious society of Japanese executives, the Keidanren, on how to apply statistical methods in business.

The Japanese Union of Scientists and Engineers would later establish a prize in his honor—awarded to statisticians and companies for their improved use of statistical theory in organizations, consumer research, product design, and production.

More to the point, as the British Library has noted, the revolution in Japanese manufacturing management that led to the economic miracle of the 1970s and 1980s has been primarily attributed to Deming. His thinking as the Founding Father of Total Quality Management, transformed Japanese industry and the economy. It helped manufacturers improve quality and simultaneously lower costs. This brought to life the knowledge Deming had gained at universities and while working for the government, and from his own early life experience of thrift, eschewing waste, and valuing collaboration.

Still, Deming's methods were relatively unknown in the United States until June 24, 1980, when NBC News broadcast an episode of its show, *NBC White Paper*, called "If Japan Can... Why Can't We?" The show details how Japan captured the world's automotive and electronics markets by following Deming's advice to practice continual improvement and think of manufacturing as a system, not as bits and pieces.

The episode introduced Deming's methods to American businesses and became a turning point for American quality control. A little more than a decade later, this approach would be called "lean manufacturing." This is a methodology that focuses on minimizing waste within manufacturing systems while simultaneously maximizing productivity.

Deming would develop his ideas into a system he described as the "14 Points for Management"—which he argued could benefit business, education, and government. These include providing a new, outside view; transforming managers to leaders; increasing quality, customer loyalty, worker satisfaction, and, ultimately, profitability; reducing costs by reducing waste, rework, and staff attrition and litigation; removing fear and competition from the workplace and classroom; realizing the power and pleasure derived from intrinsic motivation; cultivating the value and results of cooperation and collaboration; thinking in new ways and taking action based on confirmed knowledge; understanding the importance of a better system for achieving better outcomes; working towards continual improvement—individually and collectively; supporting individuals and organizations through the first disruptive steps of transformation; creating opportunities for continued, lifelong learning to bring long-term meaning, satisfaction, and joy; and addressing different learning styles (generational) and cultivating the next generation of leaders.

The Promise of a Paradigm Shift Around Talent

People, of course, are less predictable than parts, technology, or even digital systems. But if we are intentional, we have a similar opportunity to take waste out of the talent system and better prepare for the future.

Knowing we are in a time of exponential change; we need to orient our enterprises so the people who work for us are better prepared for those changes. Knowing that leaving millions of people behind in our economy affects not only those people and their families but also the communities in which we live—and ultimately, our businesses and economy—we need to stand up and step up. We need to figure out where the positions in our enterprises fit on the ladder of skills people need as they climb the greater levels of personal success.

We must take a fresh look at what we can achieve now. We cannot wait for the government, education, the nonprofit community, or other entities to solve today's critical talent-related challenges. Instead, we must seize the power of possibility inherent in our organizations.

We also need to learn to collaborate better, and across sectors, which is the only way to solve truly big systemic problems. And we must recognize that every one of those entities—government, education, and the nonprofit community—are opportunities for us to partner.

Put another way, we have an opportunity to change our view of value, stop trying to pay people to stay, and start creating an attractive place to grow by prioritizing investment in talent development. After all, as leaders of small and medium-sized businesses, we need people who will help us embrace the fast-changing landscape of business today. And really, only people who feel prepared to face the fast-changing landscape of life will be willing to dig in and be engaged in helping us.

As Peter Senge wrote in *The Fifth Discipline*, if an actor in a system changes, the system changes. Each of us is a significant actor in the talent system. We have a position of influence by employing people. So, if we want to have an impact, we should start with the enterprises we have at our disposal. As leaders and employers, we impact people's lives *every* day. This gives us an incredible opportunity to be of influence for the good of our people and our enterprises.

This is where the intentionality I mentioned above comes in. In Part II, I will develop these ideas in much more detail. But first, I want to share my journey, which provides an interesting parallel and, ultimately, demonstrates the deep sense of purpose that leaders can gain by doing this work.

CHAPTER TWO
MY EARLY INTRODUCTION TO THE WORLD AND ITS SCHISMS

As a kid, I spent hours in a big empty refrigerator box, day after day and week after week. This wasn't because my family struggled financially, and I had to create fun from nothing. Instead, I ended up in the box because my third-grade teacher, Mrs. VanderHeide, didn't like me, didn't believe in me, and hated that I wouldn't follow instructions. This happened once when she rewrote "America the Beautiful"—which she called "'America the Junky,' with amber waves of smog"—and insisted the entire class sing it. I refused. Out to the box I was sent.

Another time, she tried to teach us knitting, and I wouldn't do it. To the box.

To the box, the box, the box.

The box was provided by her husband, who was a refrigerator repairman. It sat in the hallway outside our classroom, and it was her way of getting rid of me.

Welcome to third grade.

In fifth grade, I had a teacher who treated me similarly. She just didn't like or believe in me—or effectively engage me in learning, growing, and thinking—the stuff of schooling.

Her way of getting rid of me was to send me to the principal's office. I'd waste whole afternoons there, entertaining myself by throwing pencils at the ceiling and trying to make them stick.

My reputation was becoming embedded: I was a bad, naughty student—a failure.

It was not an unfamiliar feeling. As I suggested in the Prologue, my father was not a parent inclined to praise. Not when I was a child or a young man working in the family business. He routinely told me I was too soft to succeed in business. There was a pattern of negative messages that wasn't lost on me. I developed a clear sense that people didn't see potential in me. I was the redheaded stepchild.

Fortunately, however, there were a few powerful exceptions. My fourth-grade teacher, Mrs. Snapper, probably saved my life—because she did believe in me. I don't remember anything particular or profound that she said or did. It's more like that famous Maya Angelou quote: "I've learned that people will forget what you said, people will forget what you did, but people will never forget how you made them feel." She made me feel I had potential.

My sixth-grade teacher was similar. He tried to find things I was good at, which was a doorway to developing the confidence to try other things, take risks, and learn new skills.

But still, I carried the sense of being an underdog well into adulthood.

Why, you may be thinking, am I sharing all of this?

I know I benefited from my family's privilege—from the fact that I lived in a 10,000-square-foot house, went to private school, and had two parents who instilled in me a strong work ethic.

But I know this is not everyone's reality. And if I hadn't had some of those advantages, my early negative experiences may have affected me differently. Sometimes, not having other people believe in you can make people fight back—and be all the more determined to prove themselves. But in many cases, it leads to the opposite: the loss of potential, which is a loss for the individual and the families, communities, and businesses they are a part of. It often leads to people giving up. They stop striving for anything better.

Today, it's what I see all around us.

Going to Work

When I was twelve, my father made a pronouncement that would change my life.

"You take care of the girls," he told my mother. "I'll take care of Mark."

That's when he decided no more summers spent at the cottage or the beach. It was time for me to work ten or twelve hours daily in his factory, for half-minimum wage and a double dose of criticism.

As I wrote in the Introduction, on my first day at my father's factory, my dad gathered his supervisors around his desk and introduced me. Then he said: "Even though he is my son, fire him if he does anything wrong. Don't come to bother me. Just fire him."

He never let up from that day. The challenges multiplied because we were so different. He was a genius engineer and inventor with sixty patents and three market-defining inventions, but he treated his workers as if he didn't care about them at all.

On the other hand, I was mainly interested in the people I worked with. And getting to know the people who worked in my dad's factory opened my eyes to the reality of their lives. I learned they sometimes had to choose between buying groceries or school clothes for their children. And that when their old car broke down, they didn't have the money to fix it. They were tired and stressed from having too little money to meet everyday expenses—the stress that wears you down when it becomes a way of life.

I wanted to help and vowed that if I ever got to run the family business, I would do it differently than my dad did. I believed that you could care about people and be profitable. And I tried, covertly, to have that kind of influence in the factory. But he was still the boss.

Can Capitalism and Compassion Coexist?

So, when I was just sixteen and assigned an essay to write for high school, I asked to interview another successful businessman in my hometown of Grand Rapids, Michigan: Richard M. DeVos, the co-founder of Amway. Unlike my father, DeVos was a people person. And I saw it as an opportunity to ask the question that ate at me: Can capitalism and compassion coexist?

Unlike my father, Mr. DeVos, as I called him, thrived as a people person. Indeed, the enterprise he built with Jay Van Andel was based on a business model fueled by the power of relationships. And though I didn't know this then, he would write a book called *Compassionate Capitalism: People Helping People Help Themselves.*

When I reached Mr. Devos on the phone, I explained that I wanted to interview him for an essay for my religion class. The focus, I said, would be, "Can Christianity and business coexist?"

Mr. DeVos agreed to an interview. The following Sunday after church, we met in a room off the pastor's office at LaGrave Avenue Christian Reformed Church. He was thin, tan, and balding a bit. He also seemed very relaxed—not what I expected from a businessman. He even had a slight twang that made him sound like Jimmy Buffett.

I had my list of questions, and he had his answers. I no longer remember any of them. But I remember the feeling I was left with, which was hopeful that business could be a calling that could be a legitimate way to find financial success and have a life of purpose and positive impact in the world.

Of course, understanding something and doing it are two different things. It would take me quite a while to bring this to life.

Academic v. Worldly Success

When I was eighteen or nineteen, I took a business class with Dr. Shirley Roels at Calvin College, a Christian university in Grand Rapids. She was the co-author of *Business Through the Eyes of Faith*, published by HarperOne. She would go on to write *On Moral Business: Classical and Contemporary Resources for Ethics in Economic Life*, and *Organization Man, Organization Woman: Calling, Leadership, and Culture*.

Her work resonated deeply with me—being entirely aligned with that question I had begun to ask myself as a high school student. Because of my interest in the material and connection with her, I worked especially hard in Dr. Roels's class. To my incredible frustration, however, my grades were still poor. No matter what I did, I couldn't earn better than a C minus.

Exasperated, I spoke with her about this in the hallway outside her classroom. Then she said something I will never forget.

"You know, Mark, what I've learned over the years is that most of my A students end up working for my C students," she said.

Then she explained that she believed this happened because students who consistently earned top grades didn't learn how to struggle and keep going. C students did. "So, don't worry about it, and keep going," she said.

This was one of those conversations that I have always remembered. It was one of those conversations that gave me a lifeline. It challenged common dualistic thinking around success—that top grades in school will lead to top performance in the workplace, and poor grades will lead to failure.

Bighearted v. Hardheaded

My parents had the most significant influence on my learning to compartmentalize myself rather than becoming an integrated person. They modeled two opposing ways of being: my mother was the artistic, feeling one, and my father was the disciplined, hardheaded one. For nearly as long as I can remember, it was clear who I should emulate.

Nancy was twenty-eight, creative, and independent. She was one of the roughly 1 percent of women in America who attended college in the 1950s. She attended Lawrence College, a liberal arts college and conservatory of music, and went on to have a career as a school teacher. She later went to work for Follett, a publishing house headquartered in Westchester, Illinois.

Nancy worked in its downtown Chicago office, where she focused on publishing music books. And then someone who knew her and my dad told her that Leo Peters was looking for a nanny to help him care for six daughters at his Grand Rapids, Michigan, home. She agreed—giving up her career in Chicago and moving to Grand Rapids—for reasons I never discovered. She did not come from money. Her father was a public servant. Perhaps she was intrigued by the experience of working and living in a mansion.

Whatever the reasons, from the stories I heard from my older sisters, the household suddenly resembled the Von Trapp family from *The Sound of Music*. My father was stern. Meanwhile, everyone fell in love with Nancy. She played music, led the Peters girls in songs, and brought a female touch, creativity, and a big, loving personality to a family that had been grieving.

Not long after, he proposed, and then they had me. I never had the sense that they were deeply in love. I suspect it was more a marriage of convenience. My father needed help with his children, and everyone loved Nancy.

For me, she provided a necessary balance. While my father was controlled, she was creative. She gave voice lessons and performed with a local group in Gilbert and Sullivan shows.

And when I came home from middle school after being teased mercilessly—because I was a skinny, scrawny, unfocused kid who couldn't catch a ball—she would hug me and listen.

I dared not be as openly creative as she was—singing in the choir and performing in local theater. My creativity became much more private, as a writer of poems and short fiction stories. But I saw her as a model of creative expression. And I saw how happy it made her. She loved music, theater, opera, dancing, reading, poetry, playing the piano in our lake cottage, and urging everyone around her to sing. And she got everyone involved in playing games—from Scrabble to Gin Rummy to Twister. I think she saw the softer side in me, too.

She had a big personality. But she was not manipulative. What you saw was what you got. She'd yell or even give a quick spank if she got mad. Then she'd go back to being happy.

This starkly contrasted with my dad, who could hold a grudge for months and was usually nice when he wanted something.

By nature, I am an empath, someone highly tuned to the feelings and emotions of people around me, and I feel those emotions intensely. I was also inclined toward creativity—music, writing, and other pursuits. But I stopped trying to learn the piano. I kept my writing largely secret. And I kept many of my feelings to myself.

Breaking Point

In my early twenties, I fell in love with a woman named Rachael. I proposed, and she accepted. But my father objected.

Rachael's father was a very successful engineer but also very introverted. Her mother was super-extroverted, and extroverted people irritated the hell out of my father. He thought that if I married Rachael, I would end up like her dad—which, to my dad, looked henpecked.

My father didn't tell Rachael or her parents any of this. Instead, he told her, "Look, you don't like me, and I don't like you. And if you and Mark go through with this, nothing you see here will ever be yours."

My father had already kicked two of my older half-sisters out of the family, so I knew he wasn't bluffing. Sadly, but wisely, she also wanted no part of this, so she basically called off the engagement. I didn't blame her, but I blamed my dad. And I snapped. Years of simmering anger came to a boiling point.

I thought, "I will beat you at your own game. There is a fifty-five-year difference between us, and I will win. There is no scenario, except if he kills me off, in which I don't win." I decided to bury that soft side of me, put my head down, and work my ass off to be more successful than my dad—and to build barriers so that I would not let anyone hurt me.

Being in my twenties, I didn't realize that I had disintegrated the essence of who I was—the part of me that was soft. I became determined not to have any deep emotions. So, my personal life became a train wreck, because I wasn't going to allow myself to be emotionally vulnerable to anyone.

Interestingly, however, I still cared very much about people at work and helping others. I kept the two sides of me separate: in my twenties and thirties, I spent much time doing grassroots nonprofit volunteer work. Looking back, I think I was simultaneously living out my empathy and trying to protect that inner child's vulnerability.

CHAPTER THREE
EMPATHY IN AN ENTERPRISE

Shortly after the debacle surrounding my engagement, I took a job working for Land O'Lakes at their Kent, Ohio, plant. Of course, it was a competitor to my father's business. It also paid more than he would pay me, but I still couldn't make ends meet.

I clearly remember standing in line at the grocery store with a can of Campbell's soup in my hand. It's all I could afford with the sixty-one cents in my pocket. I purchased a gym membership and figured out that if I took my showers at the gym and used their soap, razors, shaving cream, shampoo, and towels, it would be cheaper than running the shower in my apartment, doing the extra laundry, and paying for soap, shampoo, and razors. I learned to work on my old truck and change the wheel bearings and other things instead of taking it to a mechanic. On Mondays, I would buy pizza because that's when the local pizzeria had a two-for-one special. I could have meals all week if I ate two slices a night. I was often so hungry I wanted four pieces for dinner. I only allowed myself two slices because I had to make the pies last all week.

My dad hadn't taught me about money, how to make a budget, or how to make sound financial decisions. I didn't learn that earning a salary of $25,000 a year meant I could only afford an apartment of around $500 a month—or even less because I had a car loan, too. And so, I had made the classic mistake of using credit to live beyond my means. I bought furniture on credit. It seemed everyone was giving out credit cards right and left then. I'd go to the store, and they'd offer a credit card with a $2,000 limit, and I thought, *free money!* As the bills came due, I would take a cash advance from one credit card to pay off another.

When you're young, you always think you can figure it out. But it was stressful. It was constant stress and a constant shell game. I was just shifting debt around.

But the biggest problem was I rented an apartment that was more than I could afford on my salary, and I was stuck with a twelve-month lease. And eventually, of course, I hit a wall. I just couldn't keep going the way I did.

So, I was forced to put my tail between my legs and ask for my dad's help. I put my whole debt situation in a spreadsheet and asked my dad for an interest-free loan.

"Why would I do that?" he said.

"Just to help me out," I said.

"I'm not going to do that," he said.

So, I went to a local bank to get a debt consolidation loan. While the loan was in in process, my dad asked what I was going to do. I told him about the debt consolidation loan. His response surprised me.

"I'll give you your interest free loan, but there will be some conditions."

I had to give up my apartment and live at home. I also had to work for him and allow him to garnish my wages to repay the loan. It was much better than paying 18-to-20 percent interest on credit cards. So, I took the deal and accepted the conditions. It took about a year.

And I know I was one of the lucky ones. I was making around twelve dollars an hour, and I had no chance of making significantly more than that. I had a good job as a plant manager, and I also had a wealthy parent who could help me escape this predicament.

Countless people in America are not so lucky. Even those who are smart enough not to overspend, as I did, still struggle to make ends meet. They can't significantly alter the revenue or the expense side of the equation in their lives. So, they just stay stuck in their predicament. Week after week. Month after month. Year after year. Never getting ahead, and losing hope. And for many, unknowingly, falling behind from a skill perspective, as the speed of development continues to accelerate around them.

Now, before you stop reading here and think people who experience this sort of daily insecurity are working for fast-food restaurants, food-production-and-packaging companies, distribution warehouses, commissaries in hospitals, call centers, or are in some sort of service job, think again. All kinds of Americans making the equivalent of twenty-five dollars an hour, or approximately $50,000 a year, live like this daily. And if you know anything about the physiology of our bodies, you will understand that that stress level creates the constant presence of cortisol, which can be debilitating to someone's health and productivity.

They exist based on the tyranny of the urgent. They come to work for us seeing it as a job that can easily be lost, because that is their experience. Their circumstances can also make that a self-fulfilling prophecy. After all, I know I would find it difficult to focus on the task before me if I were worried about how to pay for repairs to a car I needed to get my children to school and me to work. Plus, things have only gotten more challenging since the days when I struggled to get by. So many things are in flux. Prices have been skyrocketing. Where I live, it is difficult for many people to find a reasonably priced car—or a home. And once you get sucked into a system of high-interest rates and debt, things become ever more challenging. And difficult to change.

But I ask myself repeatedly: What if we—the leaders of businesses or future leaders—were the ones to create change that made things more stable and successful for individuals and our organizations? Why wouldn't we?

What a Little Support Can Do

When I was in my twenties, I started tutoring at The Potter's House, an inner-city Christian school supported mainly by donors, because I loved what they were doing but didn't have any money to donate. The first student who I was assigned to had severe ADD. He just could not sit still. We ended up in the basement together, just us and a chalkboard. I would try to teach him math. Meanwhile, he would stand on a desk, sit on the floor, and walk around the room. But we got through it, and he passed.

We worked together for several years. Then he got kicked out and ended up in a Grand Rapids public school in the special-ed program. I followed him there and talked to the staff.

"Hey," I said, "you took on this student. I want to connect with him." And they let me.

Then, one day, I met with the director of programs, Brian Cassell. He said, "Hey, we have this little store run by our non-traditional learners, where they sell candy, popcorn, and pickles to students. They learn about inventory and buying and selling at a profit. Would you be willing to give them a tour of your facility?"

"Done," I said. "That's an easy ask." So, they came out and toured the plant and had lunch with us. During lunch I had people on my team talk about their jobs and how their work related to the tasks the students did in their store.

About an hour after they left, Brian called me and said, "I hate to ask this, but I promised the students I would. They want to know if they can set up their store at your plant and sell to employees."

"That's brilliant," I said. "We have to make that happen."

So, once a week, they would bus the kids over with their candy, popcorn, and pickles and sell stuff to our employees over lunch. It lasted for five or six years.

It was so easy—and impactful. And that's the point. Investing in people can reap significant rewards and doesn't necessarily take a great investment of money or time.

For example, the restless boy I tutored wasn't the only one. For a time, I also tutored a group of three—which took an hour and ten minutes of my time once a week: ten minutes to drive to the school five blocks from our facility, fifty minutes to teach, and ten minutes back.

On the first day of class, I would always say: "You are going to hate me or love math by the end of the term."

"That's easy," they would say. "We'll never love math."

But then I'd help them understand that they wouldn't have math homework if they paid attention, because we'd do it all in class. That was a big payoff! And they did it. They paid attention, scored better on their tests, and were the kids who didn't have math homework.

These kids were restless in class and couldn't pay attention, so they didn't do well. But, feeding them information at a high speed, I showed them that we would get through the material—and the homework—by the end of class. So, at the end of the hour, other kids who looked down on them went home with homework to do, and these kids didn't. They got it done, and they understood it.

Then, after a while, I decided to take a sabbatical. But I kept thinking about the kids, so I went back one day to check on them. I walked into the classroom, and one girl threw her math book down and said, "I'm failing math because you haven't been here."

I thought, wow. One hour a week, I could change the outcomes for them. And without that hour, they could be set back. That taught me how important it is to invest in people, and to not only show them that you believe in them, but to help them believe in themselves.

It also taught me that more people were needed, and efforts were required to ensure these young people could develop the skills to learn.

That's when I started an initiative to get business people to tutor in public schools. We attracted 160 business people, all within minutes of a public school.

One of the most powerful notes I remember getting was from a man who wrote, "I had no idea how much impact one hour a week would make on a student. I also realized that I don't spend one hour a week with either of my sons. That stops now."

That's what investing in people is about. It's not about spending hundreds of hours. It's about making targeted investments in people at smart leverage points.

It's also about focusing on the impact it can have. Recently, for example, I received a note from a student I tutored in math. She told me it changed her life, and she's a physician now.

When we consider investing in people, we often feel daunted and wonder, "Oh my gosh, what will it cost me in time or money?" But with a small degree of intention, we can get so much more back.

James Clear writes in *Atomic Habits*, "Habits are the compound interest of self-improvement. In the same way money multiplies through compound interest, the effects of your habits multiply as you repeat them. They seem to make little difference on any given day, yet the impact they deliver over the months and years can be enormous. It is only when looking back two, five, or perhaps ten years later that the value of good habits and the cost of bad ones becomes strikingly apparent."

And, as my father might have said, this isn't just me being soft. It's quite the opposite. It's me seeing—from an objective, even curious perspective—that, as business leaders, we have the best opportunity to recognize and support the potential of the people who work for us in today's fast-changing world. It is incumbent on us to stop contributing to the waste in the talent system. When we give people a little push or encouragement, ask them if they have thought about returning to school, and tell them we believe in them, incredible things can happen.

The philosopher Soren Kierkegaard famously wrote, "Life can only be understood backwards; but it must be lived forwards."

Looking back now, I can see that my struggles in my early life—both financially and emotionally—have helped me tremendously. They have helped me better understand and empathize with the lives of those who now work for me. And most importantly, they helped me know that something else, something better, is possible that would benefit us all. They helped me recognize that rising to this challenge is not just a nice-to-do thing. It is imperative for businesses that want to survive and thrive in today's fast-changing economy.

In the following chapters, I will explain why I feel so confident and introduce you to some of the many extraordinary people I have spoken with in recent years who also recognize the need for a new approach to impacting people in our talent system. Ultimately, I hope to show you that doing this work is also a path to a greater sense of integration—or a holistic sense of purpose—for those of us who lead or wish to lead enterprises today.

CHAPTER FOUR
BUILDING THE SOURCE[1]

The Butterball factory is wedged in an industrial ghetto filled with old, dingy, well-used brick and steel buildings. There is no beautiful architecture. No five-star restaurants. No downtown hustle and bustle. If you go up to the roof, you can see the entire skyline of downtown Grand Rapids. It's where I go sometimes when I need to sort out something challenging—and it was where I went one day to chew on the question that was nagging at me: How could a company like mine develop the clout and resources to help people the way Fred Keller, my friend and colleague, was doing at Cascade?

Usually, when I am on the roof puzzling something out, I look out at the distant skyline. But this time, I focused on the buildings within a half-mile radius of us. I thought all those buildings had to be filled with people like those working in the factory below me. Some people struggled to make ends meet and worried about paying their rent and keeping their homes

---

[1] Excerpted from Mark Peters, *The Source: Using the Power of Collaboration to Stabilize Your Work Force and Impact Your Community* (Lion Rock Press, 2020).

warm. Those personal challenges had to interfere with their ability to work, just as they affected the people who worked for me. It also affected the businesses' bottom lines, through lost productivity and high turnover. So, what, I wondered, were these other employers doing about it? You often think your problems are unique when you are inside your building. But very usually, they're not.

Soon after, I set out to meet with the HR departments of my neighboring companies. I learned that their employees had struggles similar to those who worked for me. They also had similar aspirations. While the HR people cared about the people in their organizations, they needed more time and resources to do what needed to be done. Employers in our industrial corridor were not directly helping.

This was disappointing but not surprising. After all, assisting employees with personal problems that interfere with their work life was not—and still is not—part of the mental model most of us have as business leaders. It is not—at least not yet—a cultural norm.

Moreover, there was not a clear road map for how to help. Most human resources departments aren't set up to handle employees' personal challenges. They spend so much time keeping our businesses out of trouble that they have little or no time for anything else. What's more, even if they had the time, they would be unable to ask the questions they would have to ask to help resolve personal issues, without violating employees' confidentiality.

But then, one day, I had an "aha" moment. I knew that Grand Rapids was full of organizations designed to help people in need and provide the services our employees needed—and that these organizations had trouble finding clients. They knew that people in need were out there, but they often didn't have a good process for contacting them.

This meant that to help our employees, we didn't need to reinvent the wheel. We simply had to connect the dots—to connect our employees with those service providers.

And the operative word here was "we." While Butterball and other companies I spoke to are relatively small, we would have more power in numbers if we joined together around our common needs. We could, in effect, collectively act like a big business.

The trick would be finding people willing to join me in this mission to do some good.

By now, Fred Keller had become a true friend. So, when I explained my challenge to him, he agreed to work with me to bring Grand Rapids business leaders together to explore the idea of enabling small companies like mine to have the clout of a big company like his. The general idea was that we would all benefit if we pooled our resources to create an intermediary organization that connected frontline workers to the needed services.

We wanted this intermediary organization to connect people with sources that could help them overcome the primary barriers to taking stable employment steps in continuing education, buying a first house, and meeting all the daily struggles people face. We wanted this to be a source for tax preparation, wellness, language classes, you name it. We wanted our organization to link everything together in order to find the right help for the individual and family.

Together, Fred and I identified sixteen CEOs we thought would be good candidates for this venture, and we invited them to the Peninsular Club—a more than century-old private club in downtown Grand Rapids, better known as the Pen Club.

We made our pitch, doing our best to paint a picture of the value of providing the services that would lead to a more stable workforce.

Of course, something like this would require some capital to get up and running. Every CEO there, I knew, was writing checks to support various nonprofit causes. They were not afraid of spending money. So, I asked them to commit $500 a month for a year to make this happen. As Fred recalls, most of them sat there with stern faces, arms folded, and didn't say anything.

Then one raised his hand and said, "How did you come up with that number? I mean, we have Bob's business over here; he has three hundred employees, and I have fifteen. It doesn't seem fair that we should each pay $500."

Knowing he had a point, I looked at him and said: "I understand. But I also know that every person in this room can afford $500 monthly for twelve months to see if it will work."

By the end of the meeting, eight CEOs said yes. With that, we had a budget and a beginning. Thankfully, we also received some funding from the Grand Rapids Community Foundation, so we made Andrew Brower the first executive director of our new organization, The SOURCE.

Andrew recognized that one of his first challenges—keeping those eight CEOs committed beyond the first year and attracting more businesses to this effort—would be not only to provide the help to frontline workers that we envisioned, but also to create effective ways to convey the actual value of this work to business leaders.

As he put it, "CEOs and executives are usually very smart people with a certain set of experiences, but rarely are their experiences what many entry-level workers have experienced. They know how to solve problems. It would be unthinkable for them to quit a job because their car breaks down, or they have a child care issue."

He realized that part of his job would be to help business leaders recognize that helping create stability in the lives of their workers would benefit them through reduced turnover costs—but also that the lives of many of their workers were quite different from their own, as were their needs. To grasp the value of this experiment, they would need to understand something about it, too.

We have been doing this work for over twenty years. As of 2023, we have twenty-five member companies, including Cascade Engineering, The DECC Company, and Trinity Health, which have enjoyed an average 330 percent rate of return.

This chapter is meant to demonstrate the possibilities when we, as employers, intentionally use our problem-solving skills to solve problems relative to the people who come to work for us. I simply use it as a springboard to demonstrate that we have been at this work for a long time.

However, The SOURCE and the adaptations of The SOURCE still need to include a component. In the current state, these organizations do a great job of addressing the immediate and current needs of people working for us and helping them stay at work through a crisis. So, after people gain stability, what's next? And is there a way to build a framework that allows them to acquire skills and knowledge that will increase their stability? I believe there is.

The SOURCE simply proved that we can, with some intentionality, create an organization that addresses life's needs for the people who come to work for us. The next decisive step is developing that talent and building a talent "flow." How can we move people through our companies and potentially to other companies, and why would we want to invest in talent only to see them work elsewhere?

Well, I was asked at one point for an analogy for this, and while visiting the Great Salt Lake in the summer of 2022, I came up with the perfect analogy: the Great Salt Lake and the Great Lakes. The Great Salt Lake is called a "terminal lake" because three rivers flow into it, and no rivers flow out of it. You might say it has accomplished the perfect retention strategy. This is in contrast to the Great Lakes, which lose water to both the Gulf of Mexico by way of the Chicago River and, ultimately, the Mississippi River and the Atlantic Ocean by way of the St. Lawrence Seaway.

There is a cost, however, to the "ultimate retention strategy." Only two organisms can live in the Great Salt Lake: Brine shrimp and brine flies.

On the other hand, the Great Lakes have been described as "ecologically diverse ecosystems, supporting rare and unique species and habitats not found anywhere else in the world. Great Lakes coastal wetlands capture, store, and process excess nutrients from upland habitats, protect shorelines, and provide critical habitat for many species. The Great Lakes aquatic food web supports ecologically and culturally important fish populations that support Indigenous, commercial, and recreational fisheries."

So, I guess the question is, why wouldn't you want a diversity of thought and skill sets in your organization? Is your goal to become like the Great Salt Lake or the Great Lakes? I think the better question is how can we protect the diversity we already have in our enterprises and become talent incubators for ourselves and the companies our talent might move to? That is a far more motivating and exciting problem than trying to figure out how to keep people from leaving.

To be honest, I have been working on this for a long time and still do not have a process in place to do it consistently. However, having The SOURCE in place provides a great foundation to build this next level of investment.

CHAPTER FIVE
THE KEY TO THRIVING IN THESE FAST-CHANGING TIMES IS BEING TALENT-CENTRIC, NOT ENTERPRISE-CENTRIC

In today's complex, quickly evolving, uncertain world, one thing stands, across time, as the backbone of any business: people... those real human beings who show up and get the work done. They possess lives as multifaceted as ours, which involve dreams and aspirations, losses and limitations, and an endless array of ordinary and extraordinary challenges and opportunities.

Amid all the unprecedented changes we are witnessing—in technology, the economy, politics, and society—*people* are the common ground. People who (if you are an optimistic pragmatist, as I am) always harbor the growth potential: their own growth and, in turn, the growth of the communities and businesses where they live and work.

And yet, as much effort as we put into focusing on the growth of our businesses, we put relatively little effort into supporting the development of the people who make our businesses run. I don't believe it is an overstatement to say that we put more attention into developing our technologies, product lines, and financial management systems than we do into developing our people.

We are constantly scanning our horizons for improvements, opportunities, and risks. As leaders, we are always running a SWOT analysis. We focus on, worry about, and invest in enterprise management systems, financial management systems, facilities management systems, information management systems, service management systems, customer development systems, product development systems, and more—while spending little time and less money on what is referred to, rather impersonally, as talent systems.

And to the extent that we do focus on talent systems, it is often limited to the hiring, firing, benefits, compliance matters, and monitoring of people in their current roles. What we barely consider and invest in are their opportunities for growth. I know why this happens. Many entrepreneurs, leaders, and senior executives are where they are because they do not wait for someone to open a door for them. We work hard for it. We pick up and read books about growth. We break down the doors between where we are and where we want to go. That is great. The truth is that the desire for personal growth is different for different people. And the fact remains that the world continues to change at an unprecedented pace. But what if we could embed it in our organization's frameworks, encouraging and allowing our people to discover "what's next"?

As leaders, we need a shift in mindset about how we view, support, and develop the people who work for us. In many organizations, we use a nine-box matrix or similar tool to evaluate people within our organization to determine if we want to invest in them, or if they might become a risk or a liability to the organization. This is an enterprise-centric way of thinking. What if this thinking was turned into a people-centric or talent-centric way of thinking? And if those tools were put to work to identify opportunities for growth and development without concern for "organizational risk"?

I can hear the protests: "We can't afford it." "It will take too much time and effort." "We will invest, they will leave." *Yep!* Yep, you are correct. But since when have we been in the habit of letting risk get in the way of better outcomes? Every successful enterprise would have faced similar objections before they began. So would every workout plan, successful nutrition shift, race training, boating hobby, fishing hobby, and climbing aspiration. We must unpack the objections and clarify the work's benefits.

Heather E. McGowan, the acclaimed future-of-work strategist, puts it best. "We need," she says, "to shift from seeing humans being a cost to contain to an asset to develop." It is only in this way that today's business leaders can wisely prepare for the uncertainty of an ever changing and shifting technological, economic, political, social, and cultural environment. Put another way, according to McGowan, in these times of accelerating change, "No skill is more important than the skill to acquire multiple skills." And the way to do that is through learning. Our opportunity is to build a framework that facilitates this learning within or between our enterprises.

This point has not been lost on some of the nation's largest employers.

As Ginni Rometty, Executive Chairman of IBM, observed in 2019: "We face an imminent and profound transformation of the workforce over the next five to ten years as analytics and artificial intelligence change job roles at companies in all industries."[2]

The reason for this, as Klaus Schwab, executive chairman of the World Economic Forum, writes in *Foreign Affairs*, is that we have entered a new Fourth Industrial Revolution—characterized by the ongoing automation of traditional manufacturing and industrial practices, using modern smart technology such as "the internet of things," cloud computing, and artificial intelligence.[3]

"In its scale, scope, and complexity, the transformation will be unlike anything humankind has experienced before," Schwab writes. "We do not yet know just how it will unfold, but one thing is clear: the response to it must be integrated and comprehensive, involving all stakeholders of the global polity, from the public and private sectors to academia and civil society."

The speed and scope at which this transformation occurs—even during and after COVID—is head-spinning. That is why IBM's Rometty said of the impact of artificial intelligence alone: "I expect AI to change 100 percent of jobs within the next five to ten years."

---

[2] Lori Ioannou, "IBM CEO Ginni Rometty: AI Will Change 100 Percent of Jobs Over the Next Decade," CNBC, April 2, 2019. https://www.cnbc.com/2019/04/02/ibm-ceo-ginni-romettys-solution-to-closing-the-skills-gap-in-america.html

[3] Klaus Schwab, "The Fourth Industrial Revolution: What It Means and How to Respond," *Foreign Affairs*, December 12, 2015. https://www.foreignaffairs.com/articles/2015-12-12/fourth-industrial-revolution

To address these changes, IBM has invested $1 billion in initiatives like apprenticeships to train workers. And IBM is not alone. Google, Amazon, Meta Platforms, Inc. (formerly known as Facebook), and other large companies have similarly taken significant steps to provide new employee training and educational opportunities.

Please pay attention! I want you to think about what's happening in scaled organizations. It may be tempting to assume it won't impact you and me. But we need to consider the implications of these large companies with the resources to invest in this. People (talent—yours and mine, current and future) will go where the opportunity is. Big companies and governments are building infrastructure like highways to attract and develop talent. For us to ignore this is like ignoring the web, AI, or demographics. We ignore it at our peril. It is too late the day you discover you can't hire the talent you need. It's like musical chairs. When the music stops playing, there is nowhere to go without more chairs.

We know the trends and the demographics, after all. The prospects of people without the proper skills for future jobs are dismal. And when you consider the projected skill gaps—plus competition from large companies already investing in talent—that is doubly challenging, because they are pulling more and more talent away.

So, we need to learn from them and appeal to potential future employees. Now is the time for small and medium-sized businesses to invest in talent. If some people are looking for more flexible work schedules and a well-defined career path, we can offer those things. We may not be able to provide them within our particular enterprise. But if we do it well, we can offer a different suite of futures beyond the four walls of our companies.

This is what intelligent business leadership looks like in the twenty-first century. It is seen in the women and men who understand that the growth of their employees is intimately tied to the development of their businesses and communities—and who commit to creating opportunities for that growth. It involves cultivating the ability to shift and adapt—or, in a word, resiliency. When our people have that resiliency, stability, and ability to pivot, those people also make our enterprises more agile. Agile people make for agile enterprises and agile communities.

If this idea is new to you, and you worry that you don't have the time or resources to commit to educating your employees, I ask that you hang in there. That's a common concern. However, you cannot afford *not* to commit to developing your team if you want to survive and thrive. Let's explore why.

CHAPTER SIX

WHAT WE NEED TO UNDERSTAND ABOUT THE RATE OF CHANGE AND THE FUTURE OF WORK

Do you remember the year you bought your first smartphone? My first introduction to "smart" tech was purchasing a Palm Pilot and an MP3 player—before the iPod. Somewhere in the mid-late '90s. Back then, I was a bit of an "early adopter." Today, I can't stand the idea of upgrading my smartphone. By 2010, a whopping 300 million smartphones were sold. Five years later, annual sales reached 1.5 billion! And today, barely within a generation of their invention, 85 percent of Americans own a smartphone. It took more than fifty years for the invention of the traditional telephone to penetrate 75 percent of the American market. It took fewer than ten years for the smartphone to do the same.

It's characteristic of what Azeem Azhar—author, technology analyst, and member of the World Economic Forum's Global Futures Council—calls a feature of our new "Exponential Age." Linear growth has been displaced by exponential growth. Now, if you are a bit of a devil's advocate like me, you might be tempted to think that every generation has faced what felt like rapid (and perhaps at least partly unwelcome) change. And indeed, it may have felt that way. But if you examine the evidence, as Azhar has, it becomes clear that the rate of change we are currently experiencing is unprecedented.

"Suddenly, our society is being propelled forward by several innovations—computing and artificial intelligence, renewable energy, and energy storage, and new breakthroughs in biology and manufacturing," he writes in his 2021 book, *The Exponential Age: How Accelerating Technology is Transforming Business, Politics, and Society.*

What does this have to do with my argument that we must begin to tackle our talent challenges differently than before? Because, in general, while technology is driving exponential change, government, businesses, and societal norms are failing to keep up. As Azhar puts it, the result is a "chasm between new forms of technology—along with the fresh approaches to business, work, politics, and civil society they bring about—and the corporations, employees, politics, and wider social norms that get left behind."

He continues: "During the Exponential Age, technology-driven companies tend to become bigger than was previously thought possible—and traditional companies get left behind. This leads to winner-takes-all markets, where a few 'superstar' companies dominate—with their rivals spiraling into inconsequentiality. An exponential gap emerges—between our existing rules around market power, monopoly, competition, and taxes, and newly enormous companies that dominate markets."

Thanks to the emergence of these mega companies, he writes, the prospects of employees are also changing. "The relationships between workers and employees are always in flux, but now they're shifting more rapidly than ever. The superstar companies favor new styles of work, mediated by gig platforms, which may be problematic for workers. Existing laws and employment practices struggle to cope with the changing norms surrounding labor."

Forces already in motion will make it more difficult for small to mid-market companies to keep up. The systems and processes used by the largest employers and the government will make our efforts to attract and compete for talent ever more challenging. Many of these talent systems are being built and socialized to large companies, which can put them to use over thousands of people at a time. When we start becoming aware of them, it will be too late. There will be a time that will be difficult for start-ups and smaller companies until there is a countermovement—much like the food industry's countermovement to organic, locally sourced food.

And, of course, there is much more change to come, including from forces that have been growing for decades and are sure to continue to accelerate in the future.

But we are not without opportunity here!

Automation, Robotics, and AI

Eliminating manual labor through automatic controls dates back (like so many things!) to Henry Ford. The term "automation" was coined in the 1940s at the Ford Motor Company and applied to the automatic handling of parts in metalworking.

However, the concept became much more significant with the development of cybernetics—the science of communications and automatic control systems for machines and living things. The easiest way to think about cybernetics is in terms of circular feedback, in which outcomes are taken as inputs that influence the pursuit of particular conditions.

For example, think about your house thermostat. If you have a Google Nest or something similar, it makes ongoing adjustments based on how you adjust the temperature throughout the day. Put another way, it learns and automatically refines the temperature based on your preferences. That's simple cybernetics in action. There are countless other examples of that, especially in the workplace. We welcome its many advantages in the development of our homes and businesses.

But when cybernetics emerged onto the scene, it quickly raised fears of how it would affect jobs. This stemmed partly from the writings of an American mathematician, Norbert Wiener, who predicted it would lead to mass unemployment. This was the famous "machines will replace people" idea.

That was not true at the time. But the cause for concern has continued. As recently as 2019, in a report about the future of work, McKinsey & Company predicted:

> In the decade ahead, the next wave of automation technologies may accelerate the pace of change. Millions of jobs could be phased out even as new ones are created. More broadly, the day-to-day nature of work could change for nearly everyone as intelligent machines become fixtures in the American workplace.

Significantly, McKinsey concluded that automation technology will likely lead to a net gain, not a net loss, in jobs for Americans by 2030. However, not everyone will benefit or lose equally. Looking at more than 3,000 US counties and 315 cities, they forecast that we are all on very different paths—some economically strong ones, some not. In short, they cite the likelihood of widening disparities between "high-growth cities and struggling rural areas, and between high-wage workers and everyone else."

To be more specific, McKinsey's research found that a mere twenty-five megacities and high-growth hubs and peripheries may account for about 60 percent of net job growth by 2030. That means if your business is not located in New York, Los Angeles, Chicago, Dallas, or the like—as mine is not—you may be in a place that is likely to see economic and job losses from automation instead of financial and job growth in the future.

As a leader of a mid-market company, it's hard to read some of these reports and not be a little frightened. But I want to keep playing. I don't want my enterprise to fall victim to this pace of change, and I don't want the jobs or the people who do them to become obsolete. I want future-oriented jobs in my workplace. I want the people working for me now to do those jobs! This means I need an infrastructure that allows them to develop the skills to take on those jobs and continue to help build the future of my enterprise.

We can take action to provide people with the skills they need—and we need them to have—to meet the changes that will come about through automation.

We must also recognize that COVID accelerated the push for automation, robotics, and AI. Municipalities and other government bodies incentivizing businesses to invest in technology always ask how many new jobs will be created. That's why we end up reading news articles that some companies invested $5, $20, or $100 million in automation, resulting in twenty new tech jobs over the next five years. They don't tell you that they will have eliminated fifty lower-skilled jobs. We often only hear half the story.

This is where a little bit of intentionality can help. Maybe you don't get to ask all fifty to stay on, but you get to ask at least ten to stay on instead of getting rid of fifty and hiring ten new people. That's old-school thinking.

New-school thinking recognizes that going from deciding to invest in automation, to lining up vendors and financing, to ensuring that you will have customers for the products, takes time—often one and a half to two and a half years. You can use that time to train current employees to operate the new technology.

We can also use that time to prepare the people who will have to leave, such as getting them some skill training and helping them network proactively for the next thing. The goodwill from this act alone will be a huge benefit, especially if you gain a reputation for it.

I heard the story of somebody who lost everything and was walking down the street or beach wearing rags and holding everything they owned. They listened to a voice that said: *Lift your hands*. It was the voice of God saying He couldn't fill the person's hands with blessings until they let go of what they were holding.

This relates to the whole idea of retention. As employers, we are so focused on gripping tightly to the people we have that we are not practicing openhandedness. That is the retention trap: being closehanded around talent—as if by figuring out better ways to keep people, we will somehow be more successful. It is almost like the more times people slip out of our grip, the harder we work to hold the others. It's the wrong response.

Another analogy is learning how to ski. When you are going downhill and going faster and faster, the tendency is to lean back and take your pressure off the front of your skis. But when you do that, you lose your ability to control the edge. You have to lean forward. It's not intuitive, but we have to train ourselves.

I understand how hard this is. I joke about being a "control enthusiast." But we're talking about relationships here. That is key. This is about the relationships between you, the people who work for you, and your enterprise. The leverage point is to see that everyone in your organization has needs and desires that go beyond what is present in the workplace. The magic happens when you tap into those with some intentionality. As Mark Miller writes in *Chess Not Checkers: Elevate Your Leadership Game*, "Most employers are trying to extract value from their people. If you foster dreams, you'll be adding value to their lives."

By investing in people, you are putting faith in them and nourishing your relationship with them. It's about tapping into that larger suite of goals and desires openhandedly and figuring out how to allow people to grow toward their potential.

McDonald's was wildly successful at this and changed so many people's lives. It's more complicated today. But when Ray Kroc and Fred Turner were running it, people in senior executive roles had started working at a store. The move up from the mailroom to CEO was a real deal. But most businesses are notoriously bad at this stuff. Our opportunity is to get good at this.

The Rise of Robotics

Robotics is a particular application of automation worth mentioning because of the incredible progress made in this field in recent decades and its growing impact on businesses and employees. After all, robotics is focused on developing machines that can substitute for and replicate human actions.

In 2021, the highly regarded Boston Consulting Group forecast that the global robotics market would climb from about $25 billion to between $160 billion and $260 billion by 2030. That is staggering growth! Imagine your own business growing more than six-fold within a decade.

This will have significant implications for most businesses—large and small. That is why the Boston Consulting Group recommends that companies "of all types" focus on seven unfolding developments that will influence the direction of robotics over the next decade. These are:

1. Professional services robots will grow from a small market segment to market domination.
2. Changing consumer preferences and social trends will accelerate the need for advanced robotics solutions. Trends driving this, for example, include growing demand for quicker deliveries; aging demographics that will lead to the need for mobile services robots to assist in personal hygiene, exercise, meal delivery, and other jobs; and an emphasis on recycling and other sustainability measures.
3. Robots will increasingly take over traditionally lower-paying and less skill-intensive jobs.
4. Artificial intelligence (AI) and other technological advances will enhance human-to-robot interactions. For example,

they note AI will increasingly allow robots to handle unsupervised, unexpected situations.
5. Robot capabilities will include the ability to learn. Yes, robots will be increasingly able to learn! Think about that and ask yourself: Should we be doing anything short of helping the actual human beings who work for us to have an equal, if not superior, advantage to the learning capabilities of robots?
6. So-called "semi-autonomous mobile machines" (better known as self-driving cars) will increasingly be able to manage mapped-out tasks. What does this mean? By 2030, McKinsey predicts that about 8 percent of new car sales will be of self-driving cars that can navigate relatively clear roads and weather conditions, simply alerting drivers to take over when necessary. Imagine that!
7. Finally, Asian robotics companies, currently a small slice of the market, will become competitive with US and European manufacturers.

This means that the exponential change Azhar speaks of will make robots a growing feature of small and medium-sized businesses. Many of us in manufacturing think of it very differently regarding repetitive or dangerous tasks that a machine can replace. We tend to think of robots as a copy of us, of a human. However, today's "robots" are more often algorithm-driven computers with voice recognition and human-like voice interfaces that can "talk" to humans. More and more technology applications can predict and serve what we need before asking for it.

On a visit to Fresno, California, I had the opportunity to tour a fruit-packaging facility using high-speed cameras to photograph fruit as it passed by on massive conveyors. It then categorized the fruit based on color, size, and blemishes; it could even determine the degree of ripeness. It then automatically sorted the fruit, sending some of it to waste, some of it to lanes where it would head immediately to market, others to lanes where it would go to cold storage for a while, and still others of a more desirable size to lanes where it would be packaged and sold to customers who would pay more for that particular size. All of this was done with a team of six people monitoring many computers and screens.

About 300 people did all that work manually just a few years ago. This may be cutting-edge today, but it won't be tomorrow. How do we prepare people for those jobs, and what happens to the 300 whose manual labor skills are no longer needed?

This is why I think we need to see robotics' inevitability as an opportunity to involve people in business development and have them participate as we make these technological advances. Instead of just terminating them, which no one ever feels good about, we can help them obtain the skills to make them more marketable—within our companies or outside of them.

The Acceleration of Artificial Intelligence

People often think of robotics and AI interchangeably. And there is a significant overlap. But they are also distinct fields, both driving accelerated change. Perhaps the simplest way to clarify the distinction between them is this: Robotics involves the creation of robots to perform tasks without further intervention, while AI is how systems emulate the human mind to make decisions and "learn."

And "the future of AI is the future of work," as MIT experts David Autor, David A. Mindell, and Elisabeth B. Reynolds write in their 2022 book, *The Work of the Future: Building Better Jobs in an Age of Intelligent Machines*. Artificial intelligence, they note, is far from replacing humans—but still changing most occupations.

AI has yet to be developed to respond to all new situations, so it cannot replace human intelligence. However, it can be increasingly used for specialized tasks in many jobs.

For example, the authors note that AI can be used to read radiographs—a crucial part of a radiologist's job. It is also used to help pilots fly while not entirely taking over the controls. It is also used in virtual assistants or chatbots, retail, security and surveillance, manufacturing, and more. Cloud and AI technologies allowed many of us to connect and collaborate while working remotely during the pandemic, proving its worth.

The Upshot

It's been said that the first step to preparing for the future is to understand it—or at least, where we might be headed. That is one reason I have explored some of the major trends expected to reshape work—and work life—in the years ahead. I haven't even discussed COVID (in part because we have lived through it so recently). And many more trends point to massive changes for both workplaces and workers.

So, what are we to take from this?

The wave of automation and AI is coming. There is nothing anyone can do to stop it. And if we don't embrace it in this country, other countries will gain a competitive advantage. But we do have an opportunity to educate and upskill people in real time, making them and our organizations agile and well-equipped to thrive in fast-changing environments.

And we in business can do this better than universities—or in partnership with other companies *and* local and state universities. There will always be a lag time with universities because this technology is moving so quickly. But if we do the upskilling ourselves, we can help ourselves and many people who would otherwise be displaced.

In short, we won't be able to save everybody's jobs because automation and AI do make the production of many things less expensive. But we have an opportunity better than the current strategy of displace and replace: the opportunity to retrain and redeploy as many people as possible.

PART TWO
SEEING AHEAD

CHAPTER SEVEN
NEW WAYS BIG COMPANIES ARE THINKING ABOUT TALENT

Consider for a moment the words we use to talk about the people who work for us—or, in the most neutral terms, our "talent."

If you have an employee working for your organization who I would love to have on my team, I might try to "poach" them.

If I have an employee who is no longer enjoying their job—and who you might be interested in poaching—I may try to lock them into ongoing employment for me by providing salary and benefits that serve as "golden handcuffs."

If someone works for me who isn't pulling their weight, I might let them know about a "three strikes and you're out" policy—first giving them a "write up," then a "verbal warning," and finally a "written warning." Of course, the "three strikes and you're out" phrase and rule is associated with baseball. However, it has also been widely used in criminal sentencing cases that lead to life imprisonment.

If there is no improvement after three warnings, I likely will consider firing them. Someone will break the news as kindly as possible, but it will also be made official through termination or "discharge" (a term that has its roots in the Latin *discarricare*, meaning to stop loading a wagon or cart).

If I want to ensure the fired employee does not bad-mouth my company—or if I feel bad that they will suddenly find themselves without a job—I might consider giving them a "severance package" that provides some compensation even as it "cuts ties between us."

Finally, suppose I need to save on payroll expenses temporarily. In that case, I might engage in a "temporary workforce reduction" or "furlough." Interestingly, "furlough" has its roots in military usage, when soldiers were permitted to be absent from service for a time. In more recent years, it has also been used by the criminal justice system when prisoners are given conditional temporary releases from imprisonment to work.[4]

Alternately, I might engage in a more permanent layoff or "cutback"—which, like severance, implies slicing, dividing, or carving, as one might a Thanksgiving turkey.

In short, we have relatively few words for hiring someone (join our team, work with us!) and so many for firing them—the most unpleasant words: You're being fired. Terminated. Downsized. Right-sized. Given the boot. Let go. Destaffed. Defunded. Discharged. Outsourced. You are relieved of your duties. Or, more abstractly: Your services are no longer needed. We think you would be happier elsewhere. We are streamlining our department. This is an involuntary separation.

---

[4] Douglas R. Harper, *The Online Etymology Dictionary*, at https://www.etymonline.com/word/furlough

The language we use is interesting because it demonstrates a complete lack of responsibility on the part of the employer. You rarely hear an employer say:

"I am sorry we are ending your employment because we failed to provide adequate training, communication, and feedback about how you did your job. We also did not manage to pay attention to your education. We knew we would be automating many of the functions you currently do. But we did not think you would be interested in learning the skills required for the new job. So, you are no longer qualified."

Almost every statement regarding employment, especially its ending, absolves the employer of any responsibility. So, what would change if we owned that responsibility—as a growing number of the most successful companies are?

For many of us, the current challenge is that when we need something done and find someone who will do it for us at the rate we are willing to pay, it is like purchasing something you want. There is a little celebration and swiping of the hands, like "phew, that's done."

However, when it does not work out quite the way we imagined it would (and, to be honest, which we may never have communicated effectively), then we are in the uncomfortable position of living with the disconnect or having to replace the person we thought would make our lives easier.

If there is something funny and naggingly unsettling about the words we use, it is because it strikes too close to the truth. As employers, we often do not do a good job of being intentional about what someone will be doing when they come to work for us, what they can expect from us, and what we will expect from them.

In addition, individuals rarely take a job with a clear idea of what their "next job" or the following few roles in the company might be, could be, or should be. This is a failure of both the employer and the individual. There are reasons for this. We need a job done *now*. Then, if we can get someone to do that job now, we can worry about the future when it gets here.

However, when we discuss our business's future operating conditions, we have an opportunity to bring someone into our organization who could grow into multiple roles as we respond to market conditions. So, if we looked at talent that way and could "see" the benefit to the bottom line, we would change how we look at talent.

The problem is that it takes a lot of work, planning, discussion, and intentionality, which many of us don't have the time for. Yet to be sure, as I suggested above, the most successful and scaled companies in the world do this. Moreover, they work hard at it.

So, the question is: can we learn from them?

This is where a lot of us need a wake-up call. We are stuck. We need to pivot. But to do so out of fear or in a reactionary way will lead us to the wrong end. There is a great opportunity here. Technology applications can favor smaller and midmarket companies when it comes to talent. We must be smart and willing to consider working with other companies and non-traditional partners in our communities and build something different. This chapter highlights what is happening around us and ponders how we will play into these movements positively to provide our enterprises and people with market advantages!

How Big Companies Are Changing the Competition for Talent

Before you read the story that follows about the massive investments Amazon is making in employee education, let me say that I already know what you are likely to think: "That's Amazon. It's not my world. I can't compete. What they do is largely irrelevant to me." I get it! My business can't directly compete with Amazon, either. Who can?

But I want to suggest that what they are doing around talent is highly relevant to us as leaders of small and medium-sized businesses in the coming talent race. It is going to change the playing field and put us at a growing disadvantage *unless* we act now and compete the way we can: differently, smartly, collectively.

So, let me first share what they are doing and inspiring many other big businesses to do. Then, I will suggest how we respond effectively and avoid irrelevance.

In 2019, Amazon—the world's second-largest employer—made headlines by announcing it would spend $700 million over six years to retrain 100,000 of its US employees for future jobs. Called "Amazon Upskilling 2025," this initiative represented a plan to upskill what was then approximately one-third of Amazon's US workforce. The goal was to create "pathways to careers" for Amazon employees in health care, machine learning, manufacturing, robotics, computer science, and cloud computing.

Consider just a brief survey of the programs they offer:

- The Amazon Technical Academy, which equips non-technical Amazon employees with the essential skills to transition and thrive in software engineering careers.
- Associate2Tech, which trains fulfillment center associates to move into technical roles regardless of their previous IT experience.
- Machine Learning University, which offers employees with technical backgrounds the opportunity to access machine learning skills via an on-site training program.
- AmazonCareer Choice, a prepaid tuition program designed to train fulfillment center associates in high-demand occupations of their choice.
- Amazon Apprenticeship is a Department of Labor-certified program offering paid intensive classroom training and on-the-job apprenticeships with Amazon.
- AWS Training and Certification, which provides employees with courses to build practical AWS Cloud knowledge that is essential to operating in a technical field.[5]

In addition to reflecting a significant in-house investment in post-secondary education, "Amazon Upskilling 2025" was notable in that it did not require employees who benefited from the training to remain at Amazon.

"While many of our employees want to build their careers here, for others, it might be a stepping stone to different

---

[5] "Amazon Pledges to Upskill 100,000 US Employees for In-demand Jobs by 2025," Amazon Press Center, July 11, 2019. https://press.aboutamazon.com/news-releases/news-release-details/amazon-pledges-upskill-100000-us-employees-demand-jobs-2025

aspirations," Beth Galetti, senior vice president of HR, said at the time of the announcement.

"We think it's important to invest in our employees and to help them gain new skills and create more professional options for themselves," she continued. "With this pledge, we're committing to support 100,000 Amazonians in getting the skills to take the next step in their careers."[6]

According to many business experts, the commitment is poised to deliver numerous benefits to the mega-corporation. Among the benefits: it is likely to make it easier for Amazon to hire and retain employees, gain a competitive edge over rivals, and it could help to improve its image.

While some employers worry that if they offer marketable training to employees, they will leave or demand higher wages, experts say there tend to be net positive benefits.

For one thing, younger employees tend to value training highly. As Ari Ginsberg, professor of entrepreneurship and management at New York University's Stern School of Business, has observed: "Generation Z is already fairly tech-savvy and is more likely to be attracted and stay in a place where they can get technology learning."[7]

Matthew Bidwell, a professor of management at the University of Pennsylvania's Wharton School of Management, noted that upskilling current employees is likely cheaper than hiring new ones. It also boosts employee loyalty.

---

[6] Gene Marks, "Amazon is spending big to retrain employees—and so should you," *The Guardian*, July 19, 2016. https://www.theguardian.com/business/2019/jul/19/amazon-retrain-employees-benefits

[7] "Will Amazon's Plan to 'Upskill' Its Employees Pay Off?" *Knowledge at Wharton*, July 22, 2019. https://knowledge.wharton.upenn.edu/article/amazon-retraining-employees/

"You can wait for other companies and universities to train people, but that's going to be quite slow," he says. "Also, hiring is always a crapshoot, and many of the people you end up hiring are not going to work out." It seems a much smarter idea to train "some of your people who work hard and have a good attitude, and then help move" into the jobs that call for higher skills.

Please pay special attention to this line from the Amazon Initiative: "Amazon Upskilling 2025 was also notable in that it did not require that employees who benefited from the training remain at Amazon." If your goal is retention, you already lost. The goal is investment. It has to be.

More recently, in September 2021, Amazon went another big step further and announced that it is expanding its generous education and skills-training benefits to all hourly employees, effective January 2022. That made more than 750,000 US employees eligible for a free college education after ninety days. The expected investment by Amazon: $1.2 billion by 2025.[8]

Amazon Is Not Alone—Nor Should We Be

While it is currently the largest US employer to commit to massive investments in upskilling its workforce, Amazon is far from alone. Accenture, AT&T, Bank of America, Facebook, Google, IBM, Intel, JPMorgan Chase, Kaiser, PwC, Salesforce, Verizon, and others have done similarly.

In 2018, AT&T committed $1 billion to retrain nearly half of its workforce for jobs of the future. The move was prompted

---

[8] Kelly Tyko, "Amazon to pay college tuition, books and fees for U.S.US employees starting in January 2022," by Kelly Tyko. *US News and World Report.* Sept., September 29, 2021. https://www.usatoday.com/story/money/retail/2021/09/09/amazon-college-program-free-tuition-books-employees-career-choice/8261019002/

after the company discovered that almost half of its 250,000 employees lacked the necessary skills needed to keep the company competitive.[9]

In 2019, Accenture said it would spend nearly $1 billion each year to retrain its workers.[10] And in 2020, Verizon announced a $44 million upskilling program—calling the investment part of its "duty" to prepare job seekers for the future.[11]

Jason Tyszko, the US Chamber Foundation's vice president of the Center for Education and Workforce, told *Inside Higher Ed* that "enlightened self-interest" is helping to drive this significant trend. Companies increasingly feel obligated to prepare their workers to adjust to a rapidly changing job market. Employers increasingly realize they "need to provide a pathway for folks, even outside the company," said Tyszko. "We're excited to see more companies getting into the game."[12]

But again, these companies operate in a different league from most of us—companies with under five hundred employees now represent 48 percent of working Americans, a decline from the early 2000s, when we employed 52 percent of working Americans. So, what, if any, lessons are we to draw from these developments?

---

[9] Susan Caminiti, "AT&T's $1 billion gambit: Retraining nearly half its workforce for jobs of the future," CNBC, March 13, 2018. https://www.cnbc.com/2018/03/13/atts-1-billion-gambit-retraining-nearly-half-its-workforce.html

[10] Lauren Weber, "Accenture Retrains Its Workers as Technology Upends Their Jobs," *Wall Street Journal*, June 23, 2019. https://www.wsj.com/articles/accenture-retrains-its-workers-as-technology-upends-their-jobs-11561318022

[11] Marguerite Ward, "Verizon executive says the company's recent $44 million investment in upskilling is part of its duty to prepare job seekers for the future," *Insider*, October 26, 2020.

[12] Employers as Educators, *Inside Higher Ed*, July 17, 2019. https://www.insidehighered.com/digital-learning/article/2019/07/17/amazon-google-and-other-tech-companies-expand-their

The first lesson is that we need to pay attention. Many things are behind developments like this, including analyses of future worker shortages, the education gap, and jobs of the future.

These companies have recognized that the future workforce is inadequate to do the work they will need to do to continue to grow and be competitive.

No one just showed up one day and said, "Hey, I have an idea. Let's invest millions—or a billion—in upskilling workers." These decisions were highly vetted and based on a careful analysis of future needs.

The second lesson is that these investments will likely have consequences for us. With improved education benefits that can lead to future job stability, these large corporations will likely have a decisive competitive edge over us in hiring.

Just think about if you were looking for a job, and one organization with fewer than five hundred employees offered a salary and traditional benefits but nothing geared toward preparing you for advancement and the work of the future—while an Amazon or AT&T or Verizon up the road promised you a comparable salary *plus* education that had your future success in mind. Who would you go to work for?

Finally, we have to ask: How can we compete? What will differentiate us as attractive places of work? How do we amp up our intentionality around talent development?

Fortunately, some fantastic leaders are grappling with these questions, and I have been able to have conversations with them in recent years. I will introduce some of them in the following several chapters, sharing excerpts from those conversations.

CHAPTER EIGHT
WHAT WE GET TO DO AS SMALL- AND MEDIUM-SIZED- BUSINESS LEADERS

I have a friend named Ron who owns a few restaurants in town. I especially love going to his pizza place, where I still see him showing up to keep an eye on things. But years ago, he had a telling experience. He was hired to help an Italian company create a generational leadership change plan. In the process, the younger generation decided to get into producing great espresso machines, which were suddenly in demand. It looked like there would be such promise for this market that they took on significant debt as a bet on their future.

This was in the mid-to-late 1980s, after Howard Schultz, the chairman and CEO of Starbucks, had toured Italian coffeehouses and was inspired to introduce a small espresso bar in the back of one of its early Seattle stores as an experiment. Schultz recalls watching several people open their eyes wide as they tasted their first sip of this small, intense new coffee drink.

Suddenly, the baristas could not keep up with demand. And the Italian company that hired my friend was flooded with orders.

Then, Starbucks realized they could buy an equal-quality espresso machine from China for a quarter of the cost, so they stopped buying machines from the Italian company my friend had gone to work for. And just like that, the family was left with an empty production facility and significant debt. A sudden increase in demand at Starbucks created an incentive to look for a substantial decrease in the cost of espresso machines.

I tell this story because, as business leaders, we must always be aware of trends and how things might change. This is especially true for small- and medium-sized-business leaders who can get easily steamrolled by our larger, richer, more powerful competitors, whether they are customers, suppliers, or simply the people who can make better offers to talented prospective employees.

As evidenced by the preceding chapter, larger, richer, more powerful organizations are already implementing practices that can help them compete mightily for talent.

But here's the thing: for reasons I will explain below, small and medium-sized businesses have a natural competitive advantage in this talent domain—if we do it right.

By stepping out of the retention trap and into a new paradigm, we can maximize that advantage for ourselves, the people who work for us, and the talent system.

To move in this direction, though, I want to invite you to see this as the opportunity it is—just as Tom Sawyer might. I recently reread this Mark Twain classic and came to the scene where Tom plays hooky from school and goes swimming instead, then lies about it, sneaks out, and spoils his clothes in a fight.

His Aunt Polly decided to punish him by instructing him to whitewash a fence on a beautiful Saturday morning. At first, as Tom surveyed the "thirty yards of board fence nine feet high," he was crestfallen and loath to hear the ridicule of his friends as they passed him by on their way to various adventures. He hated the thought of having to do it.

So, clever character that he is, Tom decided to turn whitewashing into a privilege that not everyone has to do. He had his friends pay him for the privilege of a turn at whitewashing. Of course, being boys without money, the payment came in the form of a kite, a couple of tadpoles, six firecrackers, and the like.

But it became such a booming business that the fence received three coats of paint, and he would probably have had more if he hadn't run out of paint.

As Twain observes, Tom had "discovered a great law of human action, without knowing it—namely, that to make a man or a boy covet a thing, it is only necessary to make it difficult to attain. If he had been a great and wise philosopher, like the writer of this book, he would now have comprehended that Work consists of whatever a body is *obliged* to do, and that Play consists of whatever a body is not obliged to do."

This is the opportunity before us now—because, let's face it. We don't *have* to step out of the retention trap. We can keep trying the same old tired tactics we've employed before. No one is holding a gun to our heads, saying we must invest in talent development and develop flow in the system,

But we can. And if we do, I can guarantee the rewards will be far greater than a couple of tadpoles. With the right tools—access to information, training, and smart people—we can boost rewards to the enterprises we run, the people who work for us, and the system as a whole. We can tap the power of compounding by investing in talent.

And we are perfectly positioned for all of this. After all, employers play a unique role in our economic and talent system. Our job is to add value by being "good" at our craft, such as creating a great product, developing proprietary technology, providing a specific service or being an expert in some area.

However, our enterprises allow us to make systemic changes in the talent system, starting within our organizations.

We stand at the intersection of income and need for people who work for us. At that intersection, we are best positioned to change outcomes by offering stabilizing benefits, so people will stay at work and be able to work through some of those destabilizing complexities—at which point they will be able to start thinking about "what's next?" or what "success" looks like, since they will no longer be spending all their energy surviving. Ultimately, those efforts benefit our people, our businesses, and our communities.

Of course, it is not our job to make our workers successful—any more than it is a life coach's job to fix someone else's life. The coach's job is to find leverage points, to ask clarifying questions that lead to an *aha* moment. The same holds for those drawn to bringing a greater sense of purpose to their work. People can choose to take advantage of it or not. But we can build the framework that makes their success possible. By investing in our people and encouraging them to take advantage of development opportunities and career advancement paths, we can help them find purpose in their lives and prepare themselves—and our enterprises—for future changes.

Doing this can solve another problem, too—our sense of purpose and meaning. After twenty, thirty, or forty years of hard work—and perhaps even resounding professional and financial success—many business leaders feel something is missing. And that something is a sense of meaning and purpose—a sense that our lives added up to something more than our professional success—a feeling that our being here mattered.

At this point, many business leaders retire and seek a new chapter in their lives. Some pull the ripcord on corporate America and work for a small business. Others leave private equity and work for a nonprofit. Still others volunteer, teach, or coach. But here's the rub. Very often, in these roles, people find they are still unsatisfied because they are not having the kind of impact that is satisfying, or because they are not using the skills they developed over a lifetime.

So, here's my question: what would happen if, instead of abandoning the enterprises they helped build, they use them to have the kind of impact they want by focusing on helping others succeed? Our enterprises, after all, are powerful platforms. Whether twenty, two hundred, two thousand, or more people work for you, those are lives that you can touch and, by extension, their families and communities. It's the idea that instead of leaving what you have done, you can transform the system and find a sense of purpose in the enterprise you know.

But to succeed at this, we need to understand the people who work for us. And sadly, many of us don't. We've all seen graphs and charts about the number of people living in poverty, and yet, we move on. What we never do is stop and think, "I wonder how many people I know fall into those statistics." Well, if you run an organization that employs entry-level workers, I guarantee you know a few—just statistical probability. Other than that, how about the person who checks you out at the grocery store, the person who cuts your hair, your dental assistant, a firefighter, a childcare provider, the person who repairs your car, your HR generalist, the accounts-payable person, yoga instructors, or maybe teachers in your kid's school.

I know many of us don't know the people who work for us or might work for us, but here's a brief case in point:

During my year working on this book, I met with a few colleagues for a big brainstorming session. We spent a few days at an oceanfront resort in Fort Lauderdale to escape the Michigan winter.

Using the wall of a cabana, we created a giant mind map of sorts, using yellow, pink, and blue sticky notes Then, as we all got hungry, we ordered some food, and a young man named Jake delivered sandwiches and a plate of fruit.

Earlier in the day, before we started the mind-map project, he came by to bring us a water pitcher. I noticed he came in with his head down and quietly slipped out.

But this time, he stopped, looked at the wall, and suddenly became animated.

"Are you storyboarding?" he asked.

From a young man who seemed bored—and, one might imagine, unmotivated—he came alive before our eyes. He was excited, engaged, and curious.

Graphic design, he said, was his passion. His dream was to be able to study it.

I asked why he didn't, and he explained that he had been forced to drop out of high school because of a family issue.

I have learned not to pry in these situations. Perhaps one of his parents died, was extradited, or sent to prison. Countless tragedies, big and small, can interfere with people's dreams and potential.

He explained that because he had to find work even before he had a high school diploma, he found several odd jobs until his sister, who also worked at the resort, recommended him for a job here.

This is the behind-the-scenes of people's lives that can be hard to see or even imagine. It's embarrassing, but many of us tend to put people into boxes. This person will be successful. That person won't. This person is engaged. That person just doesn't have it in them.

We put them in boxes and then find it hard to imagine how they break out of that box. To see, for example, a young man like Jake and think: he is efficient but bored at delivering food. But he could be great if his work and skills aligned with his passion.

I asked him if his employer could help him acquire graphic design skills and if he would be interested.

His face said it all. He would be a young man aligned with his gifts.

If Jake were your son or your nephew, what sort of a conversation would you have with him? Would you connect with him if you could? Would you help him think about "both and" opportunities to work and begin to build toward a career in what he is passionate about? Of course, you would. And yet, we all have a "Jake" working for us. Probably many of them. It is not super practical to sit down and have long conversations with each of those people about their future and help them network and problem-solve how they will accomplish it. That is a lot of time and a lot of commitment. If we resign to doing this work one-to-one, it will help some people, but not many.

So, how do we build a framework? How do we start? How do we make it repeatable? How do we know if we are being successful?

Yet, this is our opportunity. This is an opportunity that only employers have. This is where we get to have a high degree of leverage in the talent system. Our weakness as entrepreneurs is that we think we need to build the system and the framework. Depending on your internal systems, some of that could be true. However, once you accept that this is a long game, it is less critical that you get it "right," and more important that you start somewhere and build it as you learn. Involve other business leaders and enterprises.

One of the most accessible places to start is by initiating simple PDPs, or personal development plans. Again, it is a long game. So, start with a few people, see how it goes and what you learn. This is simply the beginning of learning about the people who work for you and what they dream about doing. (And hey, maybe they are already doing it for you, in which case, how can you help them get better?) This is less about having PDPs for all your people within a specified number of months. It is more about doing them well, and building a process that will allow you to get them done in a targeted time, while also building them into the process with all new hires.

You will likely discover that you will eventually become curious about what is offered in your community or online regarding ongoing education and training, where there are undoubtedly many resources.

PART THREE
TODAY'S VISIONARY LEADERS

In this section, I introduce six visionary leaders in this field. There is no point, after all, in recreating the wheel. It helps to find out who is already thinking this way and see if I can adopt or adapt what they have learned. As a small to mid-market company, I cannot afford to make wholesale investments in entirely new stuff to apply to my workforce. If my business were developing those sorts of platforms, maybe. But what I can do is highlight all this work that is going on to inspire the reader to *think*, to *engage*, to *stop* making excuses, and *stop* playing the retention game.

I want to help you get out of the *retention trap* and into the *investment game*. I want to hear stories of all the successful people scattered across your community (world) who started with your organization and talk about it. Sure, I want to listen to your stories about the relatively few people who have been loyal employees for twenty-plus years—those are great stories—but what about the great stories of people who left and soared elsewhere because you got out of the retention trap?

It is happening all around us. The saying "What if we train them and they leave?" will be the mark of a manager, owner, CFO, or CEO running a shrinking, soon-to-be irrelevant organization. Don't be that person.

For those of us who run small and mid-market companies, this has to be a collaborative game. We must be the conveners, the dreamers, the future-painters, and find and bring together others to create a different opportunity for the people who come on our enterprise journey with us.

CHAPTER NINE
STANDING ON THE SHOULDERS OF GIANTS

One of the most popular courses at Harvard Business School is by Geoffrey G. Jones, a British-born business historian. He is well aware of the criticisms of American business today. He is a critic of companies seeking to maximize financial returns to shareholders without recognizing that they operate with a license from society and that their actions impact society.

However, as a historian, he also does not accept sweeping criticisms suggesting capitalism is flawed. That prompted him to write the 2023 book *Deeply Responsible Business: A Global History of Values-Driven Leadership*. It profiles business leaders and their companies from the nineteenth century and after, who combined profits with a social purpose to confront inequality, inner-city blight, and ecological degradation, while navigating restrictive laws and authoritarian regimes.

I spoke with him recently about what we can learn from historical examples of businesses prioritizing profit and social good, and how change is likely to happen now: one business at a time. Here are excerpts from our conversation.

Peters: Your book, *Deeply Responsible Business*, argues that "the best starting point for re-imagining capitalism is to re-imagine business—and its social purpose." Before we get into the history you explore, why, in the first place, do you think that we need to re-imagine capitalism?

Jones: There is a lot of stuff coming out that says capitalism is evil and flawed. Then, there is another stream of books that talk about re-imagining capitalism. They have lots of grand ideas about how everything needs to be fixed.

I got frustrated by that. I thought we needed to do something more basic. We can start fixing businesses before fixing systems. The idea is that if enough businesses get fixed, they will become the system's norm.

America is almost the worst case for all of this because—while discussing collaborative arrangements to develop a pool of talent—you can already see things like that in The Netherlands and Germany, where there is much greater cooperation.

Frankly, it's amazing you got all those people to work together for The SOURCE. That's not something you see very often, except in these clusters of people who share the same views.

Changing a firm is possible, though not easy. Changing a whole collective of firms is even more challenging.

Peters: What do firms need to fix?

Jones: The core issue is that businesses seek simply to maximize financial returns to shareholders, without recognizing that they operate with a license from society and that their actions have externalities that impact society.

We need to move to a broader definition of fiduciary duty. It's not simply about maximizing. Of course, investors need a return. However, businesses shouldn't simply focus on shareholders but on other stakeholders, in the hope that financial returns may improve even more because of the financial benefits of a cleaner environment and happier employees.

But now, if you think about giant corporations, the world's Apples pay no tax in the societies where they operate. That alone is bad. Governments waste some tax money and spend it on the public good.

A broader view wouldn't make tax evasion routine for companies. When businesses launch a product, they would think about the consequences of that product. Mark Zuckerberg could have thought about what would happen if Facebook was used to spread misinformation. ChatGPT could have thought before they launched to ask what would happen if someone asked how to make a bomb.

Thinking about the products and services you provide is essential. So is thinking about other stakeholders, employees, and the environment. And so is thinking about communities. Businesses shouldn't decimate whole towns by outsourcing jobs without considering sensible alternatives.

Peters: You tell the stories of business leaders since the nineteenth century who "pursued a broader social purpose than simply making profits, and saw business as a way of improving society and, even, solving the world's problems." Yet today, so many of us think the idea of business helping solve social problems is relatively new. What does it say that this goes back such a long way?

Jones: There is a happy story and an unhappy story. The happy story is that people built successful businesses and did good in the world. The idea is not pie in the sky. Cadbury is an example of that.

The unhappy story is that these examples are largely forgotten because they were individual people, visionaries who had it in them to do this. Once they left, it just faded away.

One of the challenges going forward is to stop this fading-away phenomenon and try to keep businesses going in this direction by trying to preserve it. One way to do that is to build networks of firms that can support each other.

Another way is through ownership, as Patagonia has done: shifting ownership into a perpetual trust so it can't be taken over by a terrible company and turned into greenwashing.

How we make this all sustainable is the biggest problem out there.

Peters: Do you find younger generations more interested in these efforts?

Jones: What disturbs me is that if you look at the 1960s and all the stuff going on then—feminism, the civil rights movement, the second wave of environmentalism—the younger generation was there. But what happens? These efforts fade.

One thing that is different now is the magnitude of some problems. I think about climate change, for example. There was nothing so dramatic before. People talked about an eroding environment in the 1960s, but it was not as bad as now. Inequality was there, but not as extreme as now. Younger generations are suffering because there is a ton of stuff they can't do that their parents did.

It is too soon to tell whether this will shift. I know my MBAs have changed. When I first started at Harvard Business School, the hero company was Enron. It was the future. Now, there are a lot of people who are very concerned about the world and what they, as business people, can do. They don't think they have answers but are looking for answers.

Peters: You write that corporate social responsibility is often little more than window dressing. Yet deep responsibility can deliver radical social and ecological responses. Big businesses increasingly feel the pressure to deliver on this. But what about small and medium-sized enterprises, which are often overwhelmed just by running them? What can motivate them to think about this?

Jones: The B Corp movement is for small and medium-sized businesses. Many smaller companies are very concerned. The problem is that as the business grows, that concern tends to fade away. That happens again and again. Either money comes to dominate, or running the business becomes too complex.

I think it's easier to be responsible if you work for a local firm than for a multinational or some other giant firm. When you are based in a community, you feel the community. You can see unhappy or unemployed people or facilities that aren't good.

Being responsible is not a walk in the park. But we can create islands that people feel proud to be part of. Then, they become more productive and happier.

Peters: Have you encountered examples of companies moving talent from one organization to another in the US?

Jones: No. It's tough. It's not in our tradition. People write about continental Europe's cooperative capitalism and the United States' competitive capitalism in capitalism literature.

But again, people doing this in a specific geography have the best shot. One key factor is that people will consider this a cost or benefit in the long run. If they see it as a cost, it becomes even more problematic. It gets easier if they see it as something that gives them an advantage. But there are going to be some costs. That's the tricky thing.

You need some strong glue for this. That's why I write about religion and philosophy; people have shared values around them. In our age, which has become more secular, the challenge is finding a more secular equivalent of those shared values we don't currently have. We have a society where it is hard to find many values across society beyond some kind of consumerism. And with the rise of social media, nobody knows what's a fact. That's a scary world.

Peters: I see many people who reach my age and decide they have been working but are not finding a purpose. So, they sell their company or quit an executive-level job and work for a nonprofit. But is doing this work a good alternative? What sort of alternatives do you see?

Jones: That's why figuring out how ownership can be transferred into perpetual trust is a nice idea. If the leader is tired and doesn't want the grind, it's a way to leave behind a legacy. Convert the business into a trust with the principles embedded in the trust. There may be a substantial personal cost. But it also could be set up in a way that is not too bad; it just requires thought. And their legacy can be so much greater because they leave behind a company that flourishes under you and continues to flourish under your values.

Peters: What principles did you uncover that reveal how companies and entrepreneurs can address social and environmental problems while being financially successful?

Jones: It's incredibly important to walk the talk. If you support some community activity or corporate social responsibility and then treat employees awfully, that's bad.

I think the principle should be that everything the firm does should have a positive impact, so it all fits together—because once it doesn't, you're in the world of greenwashing.

That's why I didn't like the corporate social responsibility story much. Ninety percent of the time, companies can do terrible things to employees or through products, and then there is some revenue to pay back to shut critics up. It never shifts the needle.

The key is for one small firm to do its thing and be part of a process that will move the whole system to a healthier set of norms that are not destructive. There are many things that go on that are quite destructive: violent video games, not treating employees well, and cheating on taxes. The more we can move away from that kind of thing to more positive things, the healthier position we will be in.

As this conversation shows, my proposal is a familiar idea. There is a long history across multiple continents trying to figure this out. Some have been very successful at it and have often gone it alone. If we take a more collaborative approach across sectors, we will have the opportunity to be more successful.

CHAPTER TEN
PIONEERS ON THE PATH

The people at Greyston like to say, "We're more than a brownie." They further say, "We don't hire people to bake brownies. We bake brownies to hire people."

After forty years at this, Greyston has earned its place as a pioneer in taking a forward-looking perspective on talent. So is Dave's Killer Bread, founded by Dave Dahl, who served fifteen years in prison before being released and joining his family's small bakery, determined to impact the world positively—and which has since become the number-one seller of organic bread in America. So is Homeboy Industries, a youth program founded in 1992 by Father Greg Boyle that has become the world's largest gang rehabilitation and re-entry program. And, at the risk of humble bragging, so is Butterball Farms, Inc.

The hiring initiatives at organizations like these have varying names, from "Open Hiring™" to "Second Chance Employment." But the common denominator is that they are willing to hire people regardless of their background—such as homelessness, drug use, or incarceration—and have demonstrated the positive results that can occur when leaders hire someone who wants a job and provides the support, training, and development needed to help them succeed, grow, and benefit not only themselves but their employers and communities.

Greyston

Greyston was co-founded in 1982 by the late American Zen Buddhist teacher and social activist Roshi Bernard (Bernie) Glassman, and businessman and philanthropist Jeffrey Fried in Yonkers—the fourth most populous city in New York State. The bakery was established as part of the Greyston Foundation, a nonprofit organization dedicated to providing employment opportunities and support services to individuals facing barriers to employment, such as homelessness, poverty, or prior incarceration.

Glassman was pivotal in developing socially engaged Buddhism, which emphasizes applying Buddhist principles to address social, political, and environmental issues. For example, one of his noted contributions was the development of the "Three Tenets" of Zen Peacemakers, which are: not knowing, bearing witness, and taking action. These principles guide individuals in approaching social issues with an open mind, empathetic observation, and compassionate action. Glassman was committed to serving marginalized communities and promoting peace and social justice. He engaged in various humanitarian efforts, including working with the homeless, AIDS patients, and prisoners, and he also facilitated peace-building initiatives in conflict zones around the world.

While Glassman was known for his spiritual leadership and social activism, Fried brought his business acumen and entrepreneurial expertise to the venture. Their collaboration laid the foundation for Greyston Bakery's success as a social enterprise dedicated to creating positive social impact through employment and community development.

Together, they established the bakery's mission and vision, including the innovative Open Hiring™ model, which offered employment opportunities to individuals regardless of their background or employment history. This goal was to break down barriers to employment and provide individuals with a pathway to self-sufficiency and economic stability.

Under Glassman's leadership, Greyston Bakery became a successful social enterprise. According to a 2018 case study by New York University's Stern School of Business Center for Sustainable Business, the company employs about 150 people who bake 35,000 pounds of brownies daily for Ben & Jerry's Ice Cream and retailers, including Whole Foods Market.

As the case study notes, the bakery is a for-profit business, but the profits serve a social purpose: creating jobs for people who would otherwise have difficulty building a self-sufficient life. More specifically, the bakery's profits fund the not-for-profit Greyston Foundation, which offers services for employees and other community members such as affordable housing, childcare, a technology learning center, workforce development programs, health and social services, and community gardens.

As we discovered in establishing The SOURCE in Grand Rapids, Michigan, the founders of Greyston found that these support services were essential to helping people stabilize and grow in the community. As Glassman said: "In the end, it seemed obvious that there was no single solution to the problem of homelessness and unemployment. Our approach had to include housing, childcare, job training, counseling, and creating jobs all at once."[13]

My friend Mike Brady served as president and CEO of Greyston Bakery from 2012 to 2020. As he says, "We drink the same Kool-Aid" around talent development for over a decade.

Brady is keenly aware that we cannot, as a country or as business leaders, leave behind millions, even hundreds of millions, of people who are ill-prepared for today's, let alone tomorrow's, job market. Yes, the economy has been improving—and things are particularly good for the wealthiest 1 percent. But as Brady has observed, hunger and poverty are everywhere today.

According to the 2022 US Census, 37.9 million Americans live in poverty. We have what has been described as "far and away the highest overall poverty rate" among twenty-six OECD countries: 17.8 percent, compared to 12.1 percent in Italy, 10.1 percent in Hungary, and 5.4 percent in Iceland.

"Despite the appearance of a very prosperous nation, we have a problem that is getting worse, not better," he said in a TED@Unilever talk. "Enabling the cycle of poverty to continue just doesn't make sense. It doesn't make sense on a humanitarian level, and it certainly doesn't make sense on a business level—when at some point maybe 50 percent of our market is just struggling to survive."

More pointedly, he adds, "We cannot expect to continue to build our business and economy on the backs of these collapsing communities. We need to make changes. We need to say how business, this great force, can address some of the social problems we have right now?"

Amen!

---

[13] B. Glassman and R. Fields, *Instructions to the Cook: A Zen Master's Lessons in Living a Life That Matters.* (New York: Crown Publishers, 1996), pp. 96–7.

Greyston Bakery has responded to this need through their Open Hiring™ model. Applicants typically do not need to submit resumes or go through traditional job interviews, and the company does not check references.

Instead, individuals interested in working at Greyston Bakery simply put their name on a waiting list, and when a position becomes available, they're offered a job. Greyston also provides support to help new employees succeed through on-the-job training, mentorship programs, and access to personal and professional development resources.

But as Brady shared, important work like this still needs to happen faster. That is one reason Greyston established the Center for Open Hiring—to share its experience, employment data, and best practices and to help other companies do what it has done.

And Greyston's new CEO and president, Joseph Kenner, has picked up this baton with abandon. For forty-one years, he recently said, "Greyston has been unlocking human potential through inclusive employment. While the essence of our mission remains, the next chapter will be to work with other companies to replicate the Open Hiring® process and to expand our workforce training and education programs."

It is also critical, Brady observes, that business leaders go further and faster to provide training and development—to address the rapidity of workplace changes and create a pipeline that helps people advance.

"If jobs skills of the future are going to be different than they are now, and executive function skills are going to be more critical as robots take over more jobs, we have to ask ourselves: How does that enable us to move away from education models that have failed so many people?" he says.

"We also need to figure out a new career lattice where instead of people only being able to go so far in a given company, they can move on to the next company and the next company. That pipeline then becomes a way for people to develop skills to advance in their careers, create credentials for themselves and build their wealth. This is how your business becomes a workforce development engine."

Dave's Killer Bread

Dave Dahl, founder of Dave's Killer Bread, personifies this potential.

Dave grew up in a family of bakers, but he struggled with addiction and a fifteen-year term in prison for drug possession, burglary, assault, and armed robbery. While in prison, he worked in the prison bakery, where he rediscovered his love for baking bread. He also underwent rehabilitation programs that helped him address his addiction issues and turn his life around.

After his last release from prison in 2004, Dave joined his brother Glenn and decided to start their bakery. They named it "Dave's Killer Bread," inspired by Dave's journey and the idea of creating bread that was not only delicious but also made with healthy, organic ingredients. They began selling their bread at farmers' markets in Portland, Oregon.

Despite facing numerous challenges, including financial difficulties and Dave's struggles with mental health, the company gradually grew and gained a loyal following. Dave's Killer Bread became known for its tasty bread and commitment to hiring individuals with criminal backgrounds, offering them a second chance at employment and a fresh start.

Over the years, Dave's Killer Bread expanded its product line to include various types of bread, bagels, and other baked goods. In 2015, he sold it for $275 million to Flowers Foods, which continued to operate the business with Dave Dahl remaining involved.

However, it continues to hire people with criminal records through what they call "Second Chance Employment," hiring the best person for the job, regardless of criminal history. And they proudly report on why this isn't just a result of its founder's personal experience but real social and business needs. Among the reasons they cite: one in three US adults has an arrest or conviction record; 610,000 potential job candidates are released from state and federal prisons yearly; a criminal record reduces the likelihood of a callback or job offer by nearly 50 percent yearly.

Emily experienced this many times. In a story she shares through Dave's Killer Breads, she explains that as a young person, she got into a relationship with a guy who got her hooked on methamphetamine—which led to her committing her first crime with him. A downward spiral followed. She was arrested approximately twenty-four times over three years. Then she decided enough was enough. She had to change her life.

But when she started looking for jobs, she realized how hard it was to change—unless someone was willing to take a chance on her.

"When you get turned down on the phone because you have a criminal record, that's really disappointing. With felonies on my record, every place I applied would tell me, 'We can't take you because it's within five years. I'm sorry…,' no matter how good my resume looked. I kept asking myself, 'What am I going to do?'"

But as she says, "Just because we've made mistakes in our past doesn't mean that we're going to continue to make the same mistakes."

Then she learned about Dave's Killer Bread.

"It was important to me that they did ask about my criminal record and that it wasn't a judgment. It was more of, 'Well, we want to know what you did and how you overcame it to gauge if you're going to continue to overcome challenges to succeed. Because if we're going to give you this opportunity, then you have to want it for yourself, too.' That's what I like about Dave's Killer Bread. Everybody's here because they want to be, and it's holding us together; we build each other up in a positive way and make sure that we all succeed in this opportunity that we have been given."

Today, she is an assistant supervisor, helping support others.

Other Forces for Good

While there aren't yet enough companies doing this kind of work, Greyston Bakery and Dave's Killer Bread aren't the only examples.

The modern Mexico restaurant Boloco, located in Boston and Hanover, New Hampshire, has a mission "to positively impact the lives and futures of Our People and Our Communities through bold and inspired food and practices."

Homeboy Industries is a nonprofit organization based in Los Angeles, California, that provides support and services to formerly gang-involved and previously incarcerated individuals. It was founded in 1988 by Father Gregory Boyle, a Jesuit priest, to address the needs of gang members in the community and offer them an alternative path away from gang life.

Homeboy Industries offers various programs and services aimed at helping individuals leave behind their gang affiliations and criminal pasts. These services include job training, education, mental health counseling, tattoo removal, legal assistance, and substance abuse treatment. The organization also operates several social enterprises, such as a bakery, cafe, and retail store, which provide program participants with employment opportunities.

And, of course, there's Butterball Farms, Inc. For over twenty-five years we have also been a voice in our community to rally support for hiring previously incarcerated people. Our efforts include establishing a website, 30-2-2, used as an information clearinghouse and a place for employers to identify their willingness to hire returning citizens.

Allow me to introduce you to one, Jimmy Erickson.

If Jimmy Erickson applied for a job with you, there are some things you could learn about him that would likely make you say, *Hell no—he's not working for me.*

Jimmy quit school at sixteen because he was too tired from partying all the time to get up for school. He got a job at a fast-food restaurant—mainly so he could take cash from the register to pay for booze and drugs.

Then came a positive turn: at seventeen, he joined the military and loved it. He was even promoted and wanted to make a career of it. But his partying continued and started getting him in trouble. So, by twenty-one, he decided he'd better get out with an honorable discharge while he still could.

After that, he returned to Michigan and did some odd jobs—at least during the winter. In the summer, he didn't feel like working. Then, he was charged with drunk driving, and his probation officer ordered him to go to AA meetings four times a week.

Thinking the meetings were stupid, he had friends sign the paper alleging he attended the meetings. A little while later, his probation officer asked if the meetings were helpful. He said no because he didn't have a drinking problem; he was just young and liked to party.

So, he carried on partying and living with four guys, all brothers who felt like family to him. But about six months later, his partying became too much for them, and they asked him to move out.

Very drunk, he stole money from them later that night. He was about to leave when one of the brothers woke up. Jimmy stabbed him, thankfully not fatally. Realizing what he had done, he started to hurry toward the door. But then he encountered another brother who woke after hearing the struggle. Jimmy cannot remember much of what happened except when he saw a figure approaching him and woke up in a creek bed. He didn't know, until he was arrested and charged with second-degree murder, that he had killed that figure, his friend.

An ideal job candidate? Not quite. But there is more to the story.

He pleaded guilty, and after spending over twenty-one years in prison, he found religion. He knew nothing could take away his responsibility for his actions. But still, he vowed that he would turn his life around. He would become a better individual and a better member of society. He would work hard and help others.

In 2008, he was released: a forty-six-year-old man with a felony record and no work experience to speak of for more than two decades. So, he went to the Hope Network, where the president took an interest in him and sent him to Butterball Farms, which he knew gave returning citizens a second chance.

"I met with the HR person at the time," Erickson recalls. "She interviewed me over the phone and then in person and said, Mr. Erickson, you should feel very fortunate this is a company that believes people deserve a second chance."

"I said, 'I do!'"

"I was hired at the minimum wage of $7.40 an hour for an entry-level position," he recalls. "At age forty-six, most people would be very disappointed with that. But I was so grateful. They honestly had a heart for giving people a second chance and weren't just looking for a cheap workforce, so I did whatever I could and worked any hours they wanted me to work."

Within nine months, Erickson was promoted to technician. Then, he became a team leader. After twelve years, he assumed his current position of shift supervisor. His salary has increased 500 percent since he began with us.

"I never felt like I could only do so much. If that were the case, I would have been thankful for that. But it was more," Erickson recalls. "They care about people, and anyone, no matter where you start, has the opportunity to advance."

Today, he is married, owns his own home, and is a deacon in his church.

"When I came out of prison, I never envisioned where I am today."

He is also a mentor at Butterball, where he counsels other returning citizens. "Most people know my story, and I try to show them all they have to do is put forth the effort."

Erickson says that not all people who exit prison are fit for employment. But those who are and make the effort, he adds, become part of the family.

In today's search for social justice employers, I find it ironic that many traditional employers think they must find some new way of doing business. "Second Chance Hiring" is a great headline focusing on one disadvantaged population set. There are many resources available now for employers who want to explore this. However, the need is much greater than that particular subset.

And more than simply hiring people is required. The real magic happens when employers realize, as Greyston and The SOURCE do, that "services for employees and other community members such as affordable housing, childcare, a technology learning center, workforce development programs, health and social services, and community gardens" are critical to the success of these individuals.[14] These services are also far easier to set up than they used to be.

Here is the opportunity. In addition to finding better ways to make and sell the products and services we bring to the market as employers, peeling back the layers of our employment system can be quite telling. The opportunity exists in our homes, with the people and talent already coming to work for us! Investing in the success of our people and again, in the words of Mike Bradey, former CEO of Greyston, "We also need to figure out a new career lattice where instead of people only being able to go so far in a given company, they can move on to the next company and the next company. That pipeline then becomes a way for people to develop skills to advance in their careers and create credentials for themselves and their wealth. This is how your business becomes a workforce development engine."

Do you want an enterprise that impacts social justice? Turn your company into a "workforce development engine!"

---

[14] Wert, Chet van. "Case Study: Greyston Bakery." NYU Stern School of Business. August 2018.

CHAPTER ELEVEN
LITTLE THINGS CAN HAVE A BIG IMPACT

Joe Fuller is a professor of Management Practice at Harvard Business School. He also co-chairs the Project on Managing the Future of Work at Harvard Business School and The Project on Workforce at Harvard.

In other words, he's a brilliant guy who understands talent issues perhaps better than anyone. Before coming to Harvard, he experienced them first-hand while serving as CEO of the advisory firm, The Monitor Group.

And he heard about them long before that. After all, as he shared with me, he's been hearing and thinking about talent issues—or what helps some people and organizations succeed and others not—since he was a child.

His parents were Harvard professors in organizational behavior and labor relations and believed in engaging children in adult conversations. They also traveled with their children—not to the usual vacation-type places but places that exposed Joe to the varied ways people live.

He's also inspiring and practical—recognizing that simple things can have a significant impact. Here are highlights of our conversation, edited for brevity and clarity.

Peters: How would you describe what works and doesn't in today's talent system? Specifically, what should employers be keeping their eye on?

Fuller: The market in which people move between companies and industries to do jobs or lay on skills they already have is efficient. About 50 percent of job leaders change sectors. In some ways, the whole market is skills-based. People are hired and tested for their skills.

What doesn't work is that we don't have a workforce development system that consciously imparts skills and labels and endorses them, giving people the type of experience they need to be recognized as credible by future employers.

Peters: It's interesting to hear you say the market is efficient—especially if you peel back from the macro view of the talent market. When I think about people working for me, it's not easy for them to figure out the next job if they are ready to go to the next job. Does the efficiency of the market change a little when you start getting to a more micro level?

Fuller: My claim of market efficiency does not suggest that all transactions are efficient. So yes, as you get closer to individual cases, that is a problem. If you are in a relatively narrow geographic area, for example, and need a salesperson, lathe operator, or truck driver, if you're paying attention, you can probably find one.

The problem is upstream of that, from education to the employment transition point, moving from being a barista to product management. People say to follow your passion for a while and figure it out. That is a nice sentiment, but the data strongly suggest a lot of risk in that strategy.

Increasingly, given the advent of technology, you are what you eat. You do what you've done. If you get on the pathway to a dead-end set of skills that are not in demand where you live, you have dug yourself into a hole that makes it hard to jump over to another job.

Peters: Is there a role that employers could play in interacting with some of those people proactively?

Fuller: Sure. What companies can do is acknowledge those transitions are hard, and waiting for the system to fix itself is waiting for Godot. We've been talking about the same problems for twenty-five years now.

We know that going to college is the way to escape poverty in America. The system works extremely well for about 20 percent of its people, marginally well for another 20 percent or so, and rapidly degrades from there.

I tell my students that the process is perfectly designed to consistently yield the results it does. If the process doesn't yield the result you want, it needs to change.

Peters: Is there an opportunity for employers to build a reputation in the talent system or change behavior in a system that gives results they don't like? I've always argued the fastest way to change system outcomes is to change one's behavior in the system.

Fuller: In a large complex system you do not control, that isn't a cop-out. It's fair. Even Jamie Diamond [the chairman and CEO of JPMorgan Chase] can't fix the US economy because he can't tell young people they should work harder and get them to do that. All he can do is create a program that tries to change things for his institution. If you have a big system around you that doesn't work, your only resort is to improve things in areas where you have decision rights. Most people need to recognize that they can do something commonsensical within their independent decision rights.

Peters: You wrote the original white paper for the Talent Management System. You make a significant case for investing in up-skilling.

Fuller: There is immense on-the-job training for high-level white-collar jobs. However, there is false logic in industries with a 60 percent or higher turnover. They don't want to invest in skill development, which creates high turnover.

The motivating logic for not investing in skill development is two-fold. One is that people generally can find people to do the job. Many employers say community colleges are an integral part of their hiring strategy. This is particularly true in jobs that don't have in-demand skills, like aeronautical engineering.

The other reason is that the economy is tight, but it's tight for everyone, so why invest in upskilling? They think, 'I can always get another cog for the wheel, and if I invest in them, they'll leave'—as opposed to they'll leave because you don't invest in them.

Peters: That's the argument I keep running into.

Fuller: I've been working on this for twelve years, and here's my theory: If you look at innovation in the employment sector, they really do start with large institutions—very few bubble up from the bottom.

The critical leap is to get out of the corporate social responsibility dialogue and into the competitiveness dialogue. This is good management. It's not doing good because you're a decent person. It's about doing well by doing good.

But the economic logic that underlines the historical system is faulty. You can see that in a couple of ways. The first is that you have these high turnover stats. The second is that there are constant skill shortages. The third is that despite many market signals, the number of STEM grads in the US hasn't changed in the past twenty-five years.

If you look at this objectively, this problem is of mounting significance for your organization. If you take a clear-eyed view, the answer will be: I have risk here, and I don't like how this is going.

I think it was Stalin who said one death is a tragedy; a million is a statistic. When this issue starts being demonstrated by people you know, it becomes an entirely different conversation. In one of my reports, you can read about a CEO noticing a worker sleeping in his car. He teared up, telling me that story. People want to do something when we're not discussing disadvantaged workers, but Joe, Judy, Juan, or Juanita.

Another important thing is that everything does not need to be a Marshall Plan. You can do many simple, commonsense things that have a significant impact.

There's a simplicity in saying that we will go to high school and, say, isolate fifty kids you are most worried about, and we'll employ all fifty of them for the summer. We'll give them something serious to do. We'll have some adults take responsibility for giving them a summer. Help them realize that 9:00 means 9:00, not 9:15, and you don't dress for work like you're going to play video games.

It's about focusing on the next ninety feet at a time—not transforming the economic system. Basically, there are two ends to the spectrum. On the one hand, some very well-meaning people overcomplicate things and try to fix multiple problems at once. Really, there is a condescending concept that underlies this: like, these people have problems, and I have to solve them for them because they can't. Yes, these people have problems, but why don't we just worry about how we can relieve them of some of that burden?

Pick something directly relevant ninety feet away that is a visible, irrefutable problem for you and the person, and see where that goes.

The other end of the spectrum is designed as powerless. People who say, 'What do you want me to do about this? I pay my taxes. I'm tired of being lectured by whomever it is. There's nothing I can do about it.' I beat students up on this. Just be honest with yourself about your priorities. Don't say I'm just the piano player.

It's the same thing with decision-makers. Don't tell me how much you care about something if you're unwilling to do something about it. Reconcile yourself. Recognize you've made that decision. If you say, 'Oh, we have five kids from Boys and Girls Club here for a week,' you're not kidding anybody. If you say, 'I believe we must get more diverse talent,' you have to do concrete things to do that. The other way to describe this end of the spectrum is to say there are just lots of rationalizations and excuses.

The point is you don't have to save the world, but there are plenty of things that you can do. We can all model better behavior.

I was so heartened by this conversation with Joe Fuller because, as he essentially said, "You're the practitioner. Go try it. We need people like you to try it." That's what we need to do. And, as he said on a more practical note, we must focus on the next ninety feet. Many of us running small-to-mid-market enterprises are not doing the thirty-year planning that a company like Exxon-Mobil does. At best, we plan three to five years out. That means we are perfectly positioned to do the next ninety feet of experimentation in this area.

Also, if you are nearing the end of your career but still holding the reins to an enterprise and are thinking about purpose and legacy, please don't listen to those who tell you to put aside the reins, cash out, and find your purpose (unless cashing out is what you want to do). But if purpose and legacy are of interest to you, consider finding them using the power, scale, and influence of your enterprise before trading that engine for cash.

CHAPTER TWELVE
A WAY OUT AND UP

Eric was at a very low point several years ago—"at the edge of a cliff," in his words. He was divorced, depressed, and making some "bad, bad" life choices.

Then, happily, he reconciled with his wife, and they had two little girls together.

But he was still in a dead-end job that paid little and provided terrible insurance. He could see no way out. He couldn't afford to quit and learn new skills that would help him get a better job, and he had a family to support.

Then, he learned about a Manpower Group program that would help him learn new skills and pay him while doing so. It involved five weeks of classroom instruction and six weeks of an internship program. It ultimately landed him a permanent job with Wabash Plastics, Inc., in Evanston, Indiana.

"I told my wife this is our second chance," he recalls, adding that he can now see opportunities opening up before him. "I don't have the crushing weight of feeling 'I'm going nowhere' anymore."

By investing in upskilling—without sacrificing income to do so—he was able to put himself on a better career path. He also earned the kind of money that allowed him to buy a home and begin planning a family vacation for the first time.

"I know many men have sacrificed for their families and felt there is no way out," he said. "This is a way out."

The Manpower Group, which describes itself as the leading global workforce solutions company, has 600,000 workers in eighty countries, including 50,000 in the United States. Everyone actively working on an assignment is eligible for benefits, including access to what Chris Layden, vice president and general manager of the Manpower Group, says can prove the most crucial benefit: access to the Manpower Group's My Path platform.

The My Path platform is designed to help people take their careers "up a notch (or two)," as Manpower puts it. It identifies potential pathways and what it would take to get there, and then helps connect them with the training to do it.

For example, it charts: if your starting point is an entry-level admin position, you could move from receptionist to front office assistant to office assistant to secretary to administrative clerk.

If your starting point is more mid-level, it shows how you could move from administrative assistant to legal secretary to program administrative assistant to office automation clerk to administrative supervisor to office manager.

And if your starting point is at the advanced level, it charts moves from executive assistant to senior executive assistant to an administrative manager to personal assistant.

It also clearly informs people of the average salary growth—from $24,960 as a receptionist to $39,520 as a personal assistant.

They offer the same for warehouse jobs, mapping an entry-level career pathway from inventory associate to order-entry clerk to receiving clerk to a dispatcher to inventory specialist; a mid-level path from distribution supervisor to transportation supervisor to operations coordinator to customs broker to freight forwarder; and an advanced level path from supply chain specialist to logistics manager to supply chain analyst—with average salary along the career path ranging from $24,960 for an inventory associate position to $52,000 for a supply chain associate position.

But this is just the surface level of the My Path platform. For example, let's say someone who works as a receiving clerk becomes interested in making it to the next step of a dispatcher. My Path then clearly informs him about what dispatchers do and what kind of experience, education, and job skills are typically required. It also shares how many job openings there were for dispatchers in the prior year and provides links to current job openings and available training offerings to help people gain the skills they might lack.

"They have access to a content library with training content tailored to the pathway," says Layden, adding that the training is offered not only by Manpower but by partner organizations, such as Rockwell Automation, for more technically specific needs.

All Manpower workers also have free access to participate in a four-year degree program with the University of Phoenix.

So, why are they doing all of this?

Trends that will Shape the Future of Work

In its 2023 workforce trends report, "The New Human Age," the Manpower Group identifies four key macro trends that they believe will impact the future of work. The first is shifting demographics, which includes the fact that birth rates continue declining. At the same time, populations are aging, creating acute talent shortages and reduced labor force participation in many countries. They also observe that skill shortages are concentrated in growth sectors. And more Gen Z workers are raising the bar for issues that matter to them, from diversity, equity, inclusion, and belonging to climate change.

The second key force Manpower identifies as impacting the future of work is individual choice. They note: "The pandemic made flexible work a reality for many employees, causing a paradigm shift in how people balance their work and personal lives. They want more choices about when, where, and how they do their jobs, without work-from-home becoming endless work. And they value personal fulfillment, learning, and growth over simple career advancement."

A third key force is tech adoption. On this front, Manpower is optimistic and realistic. They identify the potential of technological innovation and human ingenuity to create economic growth and help overcome society's challenges. However, they also emphasize that as organizations continue to invest in technology, they must foster digital skills from within while seeking external talent to maximize return on investment.

Layden says, "There is a lot of discussion about Chat GPT and all jobs going away. Our view is that we will need humans to interact with technology. A whole bunch of jobs will be displaced. That's what My Path is built around: how to transition to have the right skills over the long term to ensure employment for longer terms."

Manpower identifies two significant competitive drivers as the fourth key that will shape the future of work. One is that in a digital-first global economy, access to highly skilled talent is a distinct competitive advantage—and the market for the best and brightest is borderless. Put another way: "Everybody wants to hire local, but the reality is global."

Finally, they note that successfully competing in the marketplace also requires managing risk and building resilience amid ongoing economic and geopolitical uncertainty—from the war in Ukraine to recession concerns to supply chain disruptions.

However, perhaps the bottom line—or at least the most relevant point to this book—is Manpower's conclusion that growth industries will need to grow their talent. The report states: "Employers that focus on supporting their people in career advancement will attract, retain, create, and curate the next generation of talent at scale."

"We are trying to show," says Layden, "that if employers are not creating new value for people, they will choose somewhere else where they can get the skills and the pay they want."

The Need for Employers to Be Proactive

These trends, plus the lessons of COVID-19, point to the vital need for employers to be proactive about talent—from the perspective of eligibility requirements and reskilling.

One case in point on eligibility requirements: many employers conduct drug screenings before hiring workers, and yet marijuana is now legal in more than thirty states. Loosening requirements around testing could increase the talent pool.

Manpower also conducted a survey of 30,000 workers in the United States, and they found that one-third are supplementing their income with gig work.

"If employers need more labor, employees tell us they want more hours because they are working to supplement their income. If you are supply-challenged, your plant may have a pool of talent choosing to do other things. This is another huge opportunity, if employers and employees can get it right," says Layden.

On the reskilling front, Layden says, "I want employers to engage with us more, so that the content, skill development, and training we are doing is not done in a vacuum, but with employers, so that their workforce changes over time."

As we addressed in another chapter, large companies are already considering all this.

"Large companies are signing up," says Layden, "because they care about the workforce for commercial reasons. Those commercial reasons include their supply-chain readiness and resilience. If you are a Boeing or Rolls-Royce or a Siemens, you realize that your supply chain may take on this skill development work; but if small and medium manufacturers don't have job readiness, it could be a single point of failure for them in the future." That, he adds, is why some large companies are funding reskilling efforts that can benefit small and medium-sized companies.

Please read that paragraph multiple times! If you are a supplier to a large company, getting the talent strategy right becomes a competitive advantage and a way to mitigate customer risk. Maybe you can even supply some talent to your customers!

However, those efforts are not yet enough—pointing to the opportunities to build talent networks within communities.

"It's applying the same principle you used with The SOURCE," Layden observed, "but applying it around talent. It could be a powerful way for small to mid-market companies to compete."

Manpower is enormous and works with big companies. Its systems are being developed to invest in talent across large-scale applications. This is not hypothetical. Investments are being made, and they are well thought out. As small to mid-market employers, we need to learn from them. We need to know what's happening and figure out what we can adopt and what we can adapt.

CHAPTER THIRTEEN
LEARNING FROM THE SWISS

Andy Seth spent most of his childhood in a Los Angeles motel. His parents were immigrants from India who struggled while chasing the American Dream. His father's business went bankrupt, and they had no safety net. "The odds were stacked against us," he recalls. But his parents also prized education and encouraged him to study and work hard. "I learned early on that playing the game of life with the same set of rules as everyone else wasn't going to work," he says.

While pursuing his education, he also became a young entrepreneur, launching his first business as a DJ at thirteen. Before graduating college, he built and sold two internet companies. After college, he worked for Deloitte and Microsoft. He published a book titled *Bling: A Story about Ditching the Struggle and Living in the Flow*. In addition, he started and sold a wealth management firm and built an angel investing business in Costa Rica.

He has built nine successful businesses—at least so far. Two are social enterprises named in the top 10 percent of all B Corporations worldwide.

"I've figured out how to do well while doing good," he says.

Then, in 2022, he launched a new initiative that I recognized as having the potential to play a vital role in helping employers like me not only find purpose through other people's success but also succeed in navigating the talent challenges of today and tomorrow.

The initiative, called Apprenticeships for All, is administered through his latest startup, Apprentix, an online platform that helps companies create and manage their apprenticeships.

"I want to inspire other modern leaders to take their existing training programs, make some tweaks, and turn them into apprenticeships," he says. "There are so many incredible business benefits to implementing this structure—including diversifying your candidate pool, lowering recruiting costs, and developing your employees' skills to your company's exact needs."

In terms that echo his path to success, he adds, "We take highly motivated, low-income youth and train them in a two-year apprenticeship program to help them beat the odds and the cycle of poverty."

Here are lightly edited highlights of a conversation we had about Andy's work building a technology platform to support the creation of a job progression pathway.

The Birth of an Apprenticeship Platform

"The idea for this platform started at my wealth management business, the Lotus Group. I wanted to figure out a new model for training advisors. The typical model in that industry is that you hire kids who are rich to come over, bring their family and their friends, and in eighteen months, if they don't hit a particular milestone mark of how many assets they've brought, you fire them, but you keep the assets.

"It's a very profitable model but churns people all day long. It doesn't try to develop them. It's bringing money over. Whether they stay or not, who cares? You got the money.

"But my background is not that. I didn't come from finance. And I just disagreed with that. I thought there had to be a better way."

He found his inspiration in the Swiss model of apprenticeships.

As the Swiss Broadcasting Corporation's information channel describes it, "Switzerland's famed apprenticeship system is often held up as the 'gold standard' in vocational training." In brief, it combines learning on the job and being paid a "learning wage" with one to two days of theory at school. It has an impressive roster of alums to recommend it, including Sergio Ermotti, the former CEO of Switzerland's largest bank, UBS, Economics Minister Guy Parmelin, and Finance Minister Ueli Maurer.

All of this gave Seth an idea.

"I tried something, which was to provide an apprenticeship to a kid out of college. For eighteen months, he just trained and shadowed. He had no book of business to bring, and it wasn't about bringing in assets yet. It was the complete opposite of what the industry does. He sat down, learned about the job, and took notes. He did some tasks, but they were all about learning.

"Then, after eighteen months, we let him loose—and the kid crushed it. So, I saw that it worked. And I was hooked on this idea."

From an Experiment to a System

After that, Seth started a business with the concept of apprenticeships from day one. His first hire in the new content-marketing business, Flow, was an apprentice. He also began Radiance, a customer service business, where he trained customer service agents and apprenticed them in digital marketing.

"I figured if I could teach them digital marketing, they would have a career path that would be very successful. They would break out of poverty. I just needed to bring in the business to support them."

Seth's apprenticeship efforts worked, but as his leadership team readily told him, they were also a lot of work.

Then he had another idea.

"I had always thought, I'm an Indian; I should learn how to program, right?" During the pandemic, he taught himself programming and built a software platform to help his team manage apprenticeships better.

"I did take courses, but I effectively apprenticed myself. I hired a coach from Switzerland and worked on it daily for a year. Ultimately, I ended up with a software program that would help my leadership team. It would be something that could help anyone set up apprenticeships on their own. That company is called Apprentix."

Tracking Skills Benefits Employers and Employees

At best, what most employers are doing around training, says Seth, is telling employees, "Here are these online learning management systems and learning courses that you can take." And, of course, the vast number of courses available online and in-person vary significantly in quality—so much so it's difficult to sort the wheat from the chaff.

But even if the employee takes one of the good courses and succeeds, all they have learned is what should happen on the job. It doesn't, as Seth observes, mean they can do it. So, there's a gap in learning that needs to be covered in on-the-job training.

Two things are required for skills-based training to be effective—that is, for it to enable an employee to be proficient at their job: first, classroom experience in which they understand the context of what they're going to learn on the job, and second, and most importantly, on-the-job training.

You can see how important the second element is by looking at how the United States Department of Labor divides up time spent in in-classroom training versus on-the-job training in its registered apprenticeships. In a 2,000-hour work year, the Department of Labor dedicates 144 hours to classroom learning and the balance in on-the-job training. Put another way, nearly three times as much time is spent in on-the-job training as in classroom learning.

But it doesn't end there, either.

On-the-job training also needs to be followed up by someone evaluating whether or not the individual has achieved proficiency in the necessary skills. For training to be meaningful—to employees and employers alike—the employee has to learn the skill, and the employer has to evaluate and confirm that they are proficient at it.

But here's the real rub: even if all that happens, what then? Typically, there is no record of it—no tracking of skills learned and mastered that can be useful to employees and employees alike. All the effort, time, and money put into skills-based training can result in untransferable skills, because no one has recorded them.

Apprentix provides a platform that fills that gap—improving the transferability of skills. Seth explains, "We're putting the individual's transcript on the blockchain so that it's visible to future employers."

It shows what jobs the individual has, how long they were in training, what courses they completed—and, importantly, in what skills they have been rated as proficient by an employer, and who is the employer who rated them proficient. There's something different about an employer saying that this person knows how to do it versus someone saying, "I took a course."

That's the transferability that's missing in the market. We don't know each other, and we don't speak that language. But we know if somebody's company said this person is good at something. That's literally what a reference call is meant to do. It's just being tangible and saying this person has all these competencies. So then we have a way for people to show employers they know these things.

To go a little further, imagine a future where someone is in college. Let's say, graduates from college—and their college, instead of putting up a degree alone, says: here are the skills that this person has been rated as competent in and the classes they've completed.

Now, they graduate college, and in the future, employers can say they've got these skills. They go through jobs one, two, three, and ten years later. They have a resumé of classes and skills.

Imagine a future where we would list a job and say, here are the twenty skills that this job requires; and it would search the internet for people who have already been rated proficient in those skills, and it matches them. So, you eliminate resumés, because the skills have been tracked through that person's career.

That's where the future will be: we follow people, and employers will start to use this type of system, where they can put the skills that someone has and begin to have this resumé of skills that follows them.

And if we all have a track record of what they've done regarding skills, we'll also eliminate many questions in an interview process. We will have transferability.

An Added Benefit

At Butterball, we have long hired returning citizens. And I think of people coming out of the prison system with job skills, but then they have to convince an employer that they're proficient, and there's no flipping way for them to do it. They need the vocabulary for it.

They start with a deficit. Approximately 30 percent of our workforce needs to be more skilled in literacy to communicate their skillset to an interviewer when they get three minutes to tell them why they're qualified to do the job.

That's not easy, but a documented system that can show me their skills would help both of us.

A Big Fat Collaborative Step Further

At this point, I asked Andy if he thought this platform could support my idea that employers collaborate around helping people progress in their careers—much as they have successfully collaborated in supporting their employees to navigate challenges that could lead to work disruptions (as discussed in my book *The Source*.)

Absolutely, he said.

"I think what we've done is conflated two types of relationships when thinking about talent. First, there's marriage, which is intended to be a lifelong term. But employment is an at-will term, right? But we conflate the two and talk about workers or employees as family. We can say that to give comfort and stability, and mean that. But it doesn't mean that our expectation is a lifelong term. And I think that's where we've gotten lost.

"Work is at-will. We all know you are not going to hold on to everyone—not even close. And if you have highfliers, highly talented people you can help, you want to harness as much of that talent as long as possible.

"And they're going to fly. Of course, they're going to fly.

"But if we came together as a group and said, do we agree that these kinds of folks, when we say they know this, you're going to be good? You can use those skills. You make that whole process very efficient for the employee, but you also make it efficient for you as an employer.

"It's a curated, preferred pool of places where somebody can go, instead of the entire marketplace. And why do we curate anything? We have curated things because we otherwise end up in a paradox of choice, which is the behavioral economics term that means that everything is an option, and therefore, nothing.

"But if we can start to put tighter circles around it—not to choke people out, but rather to let them move freely—I think you put something together that is highly efficient."

Whenever somebody gives you two weeks' notice, it creates turbulence, which is a waste. I have consistently been astounded by manufacturers who claim to be great at lean manufacturing and have yet to learn their turnover cost. Because if they knew their turnover cost, they'd find it staggering. I think the numbers are so staggering that they just don't believe them.

What Andy is doing, in short, is building a tangible way to help get that waste out—and create the future of skills-based hiring and training.

CHAPTER FOURTEEN
THE TALENT PIPELINE

Let's say you're open to the idea that small and medium-sized businesses can do something different—and smarter—to tackle our talent challenges.

Let's say you also agree that it gets us nowhere to keep complaining about the talent (or lack thereof) we're getting without stepping in as the expert problem-solvers we are.

And, finally, let's say it even makes sense to you that thinking about talent as a system is likely to deliver more long-term benefits than thinking about it only as an immediate problem to fix when you can't find people to fill your open jobs.

What then? To put it another way: once we have effectively reframed the talent problem we face, how do we solve it?

Jason Tyszko was thinking about this as long ago as 2014 when many employers struggled with labor shortages. Tyszko had been responsible for coordinating interagency education, workforce, and economic development initiatives in Illinois. He also served as a policy adviser to Illinois Governor Pat Quinn's administration and a member of the executive committee that directed more than $10 billion in investments to aid the state's recovery.

Through these experiences and others, he came up with the idea that it could be helpful for employers to think about talent in terms many were already comfortable with—that is, using supply-chain management as an analogy.

"He thought that if employers could talk in terms of the quality and standards and quantity they needed to produce certain products within a certain timeframe—and apply the same pieces of information to talent—they would become better communicators of their needs," recalls Jamie Francis, vice president of policy and programs at the US Chamber of Commerce Foundation's Center for Education and Workforce.

"He had this theory in his head and felt that the Chamber Foundation was the perfect place to test the concept," Francis adds. The Chamber did, too, and hired him as vice president of the Center for Education and Workforce, where he helped lead the development of a major new initiative called Talent Pipeline Management (TPM.)

Talent Pipeline Management

The Talent Pipeline Management (TPM) initiative is a strategic alignment between classroom and career, applied to skills-gap challenges. The goal is to help employers save time and money and build scalable, sustainable talent pipelines.

While relatively new, its reach is impressive: it has already reached thousands of employers, twenty-eight industries, and thirty-seven US states, plus Washington, DC, and Canada. Participating industries include agriculture, aviation, biosciences, broadband, business services, construction, customer service, cybersecurity, data science, education, energy, entertainment, equine, financial services, food production, healthcare, hospitality, information technology, manufacturing, maritime, older adult services, petrochemical, public sector and government services, supply chain, telecommunications, trades, and transportation and logistics. Whew!

So, how does it work?

How It Works

The Chamber Foundation's Francis describes the Talent Pipeline Management model as an initiative that is "kind of in-between education and business."

Chambers, workforce boards, departments of commerce, and the like operate as hosts who bring together employers, educators, and other stakeholders for an introduction to TPM and an exploration of whether it is a good fit for one's community.

From there, the hosts lead participants through a framework that includes these six strategic steps:

1. *Organize Employer Collaboratives*

    Create a collaborative that organizes employers to identify the most critical workforce needs.

2. *Engage in Demand Planning*

    Develop projections for job openings to accurately determine the type of talent and how much of it employers would need.

3. *Communicate Competency & Credential Requirements*

    Create a shared language to better communicate competency, skills, credentialing, and other hiring requirements of critical jobs in ways that allow employers to signal similarities and differences.

4. *Analyze Talent Flows*

   Identify where employers historically source their most qualified talent and analyze the capacity of those and untapped talent sources to meet projected demand.

5. *Build Talent Supply Chains*

   Build and manage talent performance to create a positive return on investment for all partners.

6. *Continuous Improvement*

   Use data from the talent supply change to identify the most promising improvement opportunities to generate a better return on investment in the future.[15]

The US Chamber of Commerce Foundation has also developed a comprehensive curriculum, TPM Academy, and an online learning platform. As of this writing, approximately one thousand people have gone through the Academy across forty-three states and four counties. More than three thousand employers have become involved in TPM implementation efforts across thirty industries. There is also a robust community to support the work.

As Jamie Francis, who oversees the day-to-day operations of TPM, says: "It's not about you completing the training. Now, good luck on your own! We've created an amazing network with many learnings from one community to another.

---

[15] "TPM Orientation," TPM Academy, US Chamber of Commerce Foundation, 2019. https://tpmacademy.uschamberfoundation.org/wp-content/uploads/2019/10/TPM_Strategy0_FINAL.pdf

"People tell us," she adds, "that it is so helpful to have all of these people they can turn to who speak the same language and can help with strategies and overcoming obstacles."

Some businesses, of course, have asked how TPM differs from other workforce development efforts. She responds rhetorically: "Do you have any talent problems?" Her point is that so many employers face talent issues—from turnover to unfilled openings, to exorbitant onboarding and training costs, to difficulty meeting workforce diversity goals, to a lack of career advancement opportunities—it makes sense to consider a different approach than what has been tried before.

Engaging Employers as Better Communicators of Their Needs

While this overview will give you a brief sense of the framework, my point in dedicating a chapter to the Talent Pipeline Management initiative is to drive home the importance of engaging employers in addressing our talent problems.

"I think everyone would agree that a lot of the challenges that we experience stem from a huge communication issue," says Francis. "We want to equip business communities better to be clear communicators of what they need. Employers have amazing data at their fingertips. The question is, how do we leverage that in a way that helps their ROI?"

The Chamber Foundation's answer is that businesses need to not only take a seat at the table but take a leadership role in the conversation.

Doing so as collaborators gives the leaders of small and medium-sized businesses an opportunity to increase their leverage. If fifteen of us come together, for example, and engage schools and colleges around what we need, they are much more likely to listen than if one of us does.

But What About Collaborating with Competitors?

Of course, collaborating with your competitors on talent may seem a little dicey—especially to those concerned about a competitor trying to poach your talent. But there are ways to navigate these tensions.

The Chamber addresses this through what they refer to as a "therapy session." It's a time when they encourage employers to put their cards on the table and express their concerns so that they can be acknowledged and addressed. Only by talking about these obstacles, after all, can we get past the awkwardness and find solutions.

That said, it would be silly to think that everybody is equipped to be a good collaborator—or can be trusted. The practical solution is to start with employers you feel you can work with.

Here is a brief sampling of various communities where employers have found it helpful to collaborate around talent.

Case Study: The Home of Ben & Jerry's

Vermont is not the largest American state. In fact, by population, it ranks among the smallest, second only to Wyoming. Its nickname—the Green Mountain State—might give you a hint that it is rich in nature but a little less so in people. Its population of approximately 623,000 is roughly the size of a medium-sized city.

It is also home to many innovative companies. *Forbes* named Burlington one of the top ten tech hubs in the country. Yet the state's active workforce is only about 325,000—and declining. According to the Vermont Chamber of Commerce, it has a talent gap of about 11,000 workers.[16]

So, in 2016, the Vermont Business Roundtable began convening educators and employers to create a talent pipeline system that would give employers a much bigger platform for expressing their talent needs.

For example, they introduced a talent supply chain approach in the construction industry, and within months, the operation expanded to education providers statewide. It later expanded to include the healthcare and manufacturing industries, as well.

The result: by engaging in Talent Pipeline Management, employers were able to develop a consensus on the most critical jobs, forecast future needs, and create a detailed "demand plan" for talent. This gave educators much better information to respond to, enabling them to adjust their programs to better meet that demand.[17]

Case Study: The Energy Capital of the World

At the other end of the spectrum is Houston, Texas—the fourth largest city by population in the United States and one with an economy as large as a state! It is home to approximately seven million people, and its labor force is more than three million people strong. It is the headquarters for Fortune 500 companies,

---

[16] "Committing Statewide to a Strong Talent Pipeline," US Chamber of Commerce Foundation, April 24, 2019. https://www.uschamberfoundation.org/workforce/committing-statewide-to-a-strong-talent-pipeline

[17] Ibid.

including Phillips 66, Sysco, Hewlett Packard Enterprise, ConocoPhillips, and Halliburton.

But what Houston is perhaps best known for is being "the energy capital of the world." It is home to 4,600 energy companies and employs one out of three Americans who work in the field of oil and gas extraction.[18]

So, when America's great natural gas boom started to take off in 2006, Houston felt it.

"We started to confront a significant skills gap in 2012–2013," recalls Peter Beard, senior vice president for Regional Workforce Development at the Greater Houston Partnership, the region's principal business organization.

"There was a desire for us to figure out how to address that critical challenge to try to get workers needed in the petrochemicals, construction, healthcare, and the transportation sectors for positions that don't necessarily require a four-year degree," he said.

He explains that part of what they had to address was the need for more consistent training programs in schools and community colleges that would meet those needs. Another issue they had to address was the belief that the only pathway to success was a four-year college degree.

The Greater Houston Partnership recruited Beard to tackle this challenge, and he soon came across the US Chamber Foundation's thinking about seeing talent challenges as one would a supply-chain problem.

"It resonated with me," he recalls, "because it would resonate with business." Talent Pipeline Management, he explains,

---

[18] "Energy" section, Greater Houston Partnership website. https://www.houston.org/why-houston/industries/energy

reframes the issue so businesses and employers can recognize that if they address these challenges together, they could all benefit.

In other words, it creates an alternative pathway to "paying fifty cents more to steal someone you trained," Beard says, "and it increases efficiency and effectiveness for everyone."

His recommendation for others considering such efforts: "If you want a talent effort to be employer-led, start by engaging employers and getting them to work together." Beard started with one sector at a time, had them articulate their needs, and then brought significant school districts and other community partners in the room.

To those not considering such an effort, Beard offers a cautionary observation.

"If I am a big company and can increase wages to attract talent, small and medium-sized businesses are hugely disadvantaged because they have much tighter margins."

Large companies can also make significant investments in paying for college education, for example, because they recognize that it will help them maintain frontline workers for longer periods, which saves tremendously on turnover costs. He says that bodes trouble for small and medium-sized businesses unless they consider other ways to compete.

For example, says Beard, if you are a small or medium-sized employer, it's worth asking: Do you understand the workforce enough to make it worth their while to be loyal? Are there ways to provide benefits for growth? Are there adjacencies where you can be a pipeline to someone else?

In other words, small and medium businesses can act on both culture and collaboration. One possibility, says Beard: "What if small and medium-sized businesses created a human resources cooperative that hired the right talent, did the right training, and developed folks as a shared service, rather than within each of their companies?"

It's an idea we will return to.

Case Study: Home of Year-Round Sunshine (and Too Few Nurses)

America is currently facing the worst nursing shortage in history—due to an aging population, rising demand for specialty care, too few educators, and burnout.[19] The World Health Organization forecasts that the world may be short 5.7 million nurses by 2030.[20] This places extraordinary stress on today's working nurses, which increases the risk of mistakes, such as over or under-medicating patients.[21]

This is a serious concern in many places—including states that attract many retirees, such as Arizona—for health and economic reasons. The health reasons are apparent: too few nurses equals too little care to meet demand.

The economic reasons are also clear: too little supply forces hospitals to hire traveling nurses and pay overtime, which is very costly. In addition to the costs of orientation, education, and so on, a hospital can cost about $170,000 for each new nurse they

---

[19] "The 2021 American Nursing Shortage: A Data Study," University of St. Augustine for Health Sciences, May 25, 2021. https://www.usa.edu/blog/nursing-shortage/

[20] Mackenzie Bean, "World may be short 5.7M nurses by 2030: 4 report takeaways," *Becker's Hospital Review*, April 9, 2020. https://www.beckershospitalreview.com/nursing/world-may-be-short-5-7m-nurses-by-2030-4-report-takeaways.html

[21] Pascale Caravon and Ayse P. Gurses, "Nursing Workload and Patient Safety—A Human Factors Engineering Perspective," in R.G. Hughes, ed., *Patient Safety and Quality: An Evidence-Based Handbook for Nurses* (Rockville, MD: US Agency for Healthcare Research and Quality, April 2008). https://www.ncbi.nlm.nih.gov/books/NBK2657/

hire, according to the US Chamber's Talent Forward's Hospital Workforce Collaborative.[22]

However, with the help of the Phoenix Chamber of Commerce, a new, more efficient process to upskill candidates from entry to specialty nursing roles was developed in the region. Using the Talent Pipeline Management model, they worked on identifying areas of greatest need and developing a plan to meet them, to help all develop and retain nurses in the most needed specialty areas.

The employer collaborative, in turn, established a partnership with the Maricopa County Community College District to inform the curriculum across the district's ten community colleges that would best meet demand. The state approved a $5.8 million budget request to expand nursing programs—specifically focused on upskilling existing employees.

"Labor market data tell you there are the job postings out there—and they are typically understated, as was the case with nurses," says Jennifer Mellor, chief innovation officer of the Greater Phoenix Chamber.

"We were able to conduct a demand planning survey and identify the need for specialty nurses and demand," she says. "Community colleges then used that data when going to the legislature and asking for funding."

That, she adds, is one of the leverage advantages that emerge when employers collaborate.

---

[22] "Sustainable, Scalable Upskilling in Specialty Nursing," US Chamber of Commerce Foundation, September 3, 2019. https://www.forwardontalent.org/stories/hospital-workforce-collaborative/

A Great Tool with More Potential

As I see it, the Talent Pipeline Management model is a great tool, but only one piece of a holistic solution to our present talent challenges as we build a more robust response to them. It is enterprise-centric, not people-centric. The best solution is both/and.

Currently, however, TPM is limited to what employers need to do to secure talent, and it provides chambers of commerce and workforce development boards with the language to use with businesses that helps them think of the talent supply as they would their supply chain of anything else—that is, as a pipeline embedded in a system.

For example, at Butterball, we buy vanilla for our butter products. Some of our customers want inexpensive vanilla and are OK with imitation vanilla. Others want super-high-end vanilla that you can prove came from Tahiti, which requires much more complex forecasting about demand, supply, and delivery timelines. TPM applies this sort of disciplined rigor to talent planning.

But while this is super-helpful, it is very employer-need-centered and does not wander far into the complexities that derail much of our talent. It also doesn't yet push far enough into the need for us to be highly engaged in upskilling, education, and career pathways for people who work for us.

If we applied the same rigor to ensuring the success of individuals within the organization, we could develop authentic, actionable future pathways for people who come to work for us.

In short, we need to use models like TPM to focus on getting talent into open positions and creating a talent flow that supports career progressions.

CHAPTER FIFTEEN
R.I.S.E. UP

The R.I.S.E. UP Program is a powerful example of a business that has put the principles of this book into practice. This collaboration of organizations brings people into healthcare jobs who wouldn't typically have had the resources, network, or skill set to get employment in healthcare settings. One of the key leaders in this is Alison Freas, president and CEO of The SOURCE. We spoke about how she came to this work, the organizations' commitment to addressing generational poverty in the community, and how it's working. Here's what she had to say:

The first five years of my career, I was a business educator and then spent ten years in HR roles that were very focused on talent development. Whether it is high school students or adults of various ages, I'm all about trying to help people figure out what they want to do with their lives.

I've learned over the years, specifically with youth, that when they think about what they want to be when they grow up, their imagination for what is possible can be limited by what is familiar. They know what mom and dad do, they know what grandma and grandpa and other extended family members do, and maybe the jobs their neighbors or their friends' parents do.

They know certain professions exist, such as lawyers, doctors, police officers, and teachers, but there is not always an awareness of all the possibilities within those fields or beyond those roles.

With adults, particularly those who are early in their careers, I've seen how people don't necessarily know what they want to do— but the reality is that they have bills to pay. They get into a job because it is available and might work there for ten to twenty years while they raise a family, not really worrying so much about if the job itself brings them satisfaction or is the best use of their skills because they're focused on their family and keeping their bills paid.

I've seen time and again how, at some point down the line, people recognize how much they want their jobs to be a good fit for them. They want some level of satisfaction or alignment beyond paying bills. They're ready to make a move, whether that be to a different field, a different employer, or a different level of responsibility.

However, with both youth and adults, there can be confusion or misconceptions around knowing what is even a good fit.

This is why when I was introduced to the R.I.S.E. UP program, I thought it was such a genius system.

Establishing R.I.S.E. UP

R.I.S.E. UP began as a partnership between West Michigan's workforce development agency, a local healthcare system, and The SOURCE, the non-profit employee support organization that I now lead. The program uses a seven-step career pathway process to support entry-level employees in building career pathways into the healthcare industry. The workforce development agency identifies individuals interested in the healthcare industry and connects them with an employer. The SOURCE provides wrap-around support to both job seekers and incumbent workers engaging in this program to ensure that barriers to success are addressed and removed.

How it Works

Often, employers will frame entry level roles as an invitation to "come and grow with us." Less often, however, have they done the intentional, deliberate work of building out a roadmap for growth tailored to both the individual and the company. That's where this program comes in.

R.I.S.E. UP combines a career exploration and career coaching element with standard job placement practices to help folks in the community seeking employment opportunities. Instead of just getting them connected to a job, we are leveraging these partnerships to get potential employees connected to an employer that has already taken the time to map out how somebody could progress inside their organization.

What makes this really unique is the progression pathway is mapped out, documented, and communicated to employees when they begin their roles. They are given a clear outline of how they will be able to move up given time and other outlined benchmarks such as education or skill development.

We've seen how an employee who comes in and is immediately connected to a role that they know is the first step on a defined pathway is much more likely to show up every day, be productive, and focus on keeping absences to a minimum. This benefits both the employee and the business.

The employer can also be confident in their growth plans for new employees, because the employees themselves have done career coaching and job assessments that allowed them to identify how well they might align with roles in the healthcare industry they may not have previously considered.

Additionally, this approach works well for existing employees who may fit better in different roles within the industry and allows the company to retain talent by giving them a map to move people towards better aligned positions, reducing the risk of high turnover.

Another core component of this work was resource navigation. The SOURCE provided wrap-around support to program participants to ensure that barriers such as a flat tire, need for a new childcare provider, a problem with housing, did not get in the way of the forward progress they were making. Participants were introduced to the resource navigator after their first career coaching session so that they were aware of the support. Approximately 40 percent of program participants worked with the resource navigator to overcome a barrier and the program evaluation data shows that these participants were three times more likely to experience a positive employment outcome.

When employees feel empowered with knowledge about themselves and their strengths, and employers are deliberate about developing people to reach their full potential within the company, everyone wins. The access to career coaching and the system of internal career mapping make a massive impact on both employee and company success.

A Clear Business Case

What is the result of all of this?

In its pilot phase in Grand Rapids, R.I.S.E. UP boasted 479 total participants: 188 external job seekers and 238 internal employees engaging in career coaching. Of these participants, fifty-eight external job seekers were hired in and fifty-nine internal employees were promoted. These metrics were achieved in a healthcare system during the global COVID-19 pandemic and demonstrated such positive implications for the company that the employer has continued the work and is working to spread to their locations nationwide.

Another notable result was an increase in diversity coming into the organization through this qualified referral process. The intentionality of having career pathways mapped out and communicated, as well as access to resource navigation, supported all participants and helped to naturally increase diverse representation into higher levels of employment.

This increase in diversity creates a better representation of the community served by the healthcare industry and builds trust within the local community, which benefits everyone. This program has shown how when a company is intentional about reviewing their systems, removing barriers to access, and providing straightforward pathways for growth and success, the result is an internal pipeline providing committed, qualified, and diverse talent to higher level roles in the organization.

When we looked at a one-time snapshot of the wage impact for those individuals, the total was 1.1 million dollars in additional earnings. Astounding really! These numbers give us a glimpse into the impact this kind of work can have on the stability of talent for the organization, the economic participation of the individuals, and the reinvestment in the community.

In Grand Rapids, the 2.0 version of this work has begun. After we proved the model worked, we began to focus on how to scale it. Intentional partnerships have been fostered with community based organizations who can in turn refer their clients to the program. This helps to create a larger pool of job seekers. Additionally, more employer partners have been invited to participate, including industries such as manufacturing and construction, in an effort to broaden the opportunities for job seekers. We set a goal to work with 460 unique participants with an ultimate goal of influencing employer behavior to adopt formal career pathways and intentional internal work to help employees grow. These goals have potential to create over $60 million in local economic impact over the next five years.

The R.I.S.E. UP Program is an inspiration to all of us that this work is possible and has huge benefits for all involved. Imagine what could be possible if as employers we all began looking at our current talent as our future talent. With a small degree of intentionality and a little bit of work, we can all do this. Building infrastructure to do this in our enterprises is how we will be able to compete for great talent and stay out of the retention trap!

PART FOUR
SUCCEEDING

CHAPTER SIXTEEN
REDEFINING SUCCESS

I recently sat with fellow CEOs and entrepreneurs, sharing stories about companies that had grown and sold for millions of dollars. One built a company of two hundred employees and then sold it for $50 million. Another sold his for $200 million. I thought, wow, I've been working hard in business, but I've never done anything like that. And I began to feel a little inadequate.

Yes, Butterball Farms has grown significantly over the thirty years I have had the opportunity to run it, but I have not sold any enterprise for millions. I have bought and sold a few companies and started a few companies, and each time, I learned a lot and was grateful to have exited most of those ventures with modest gains or losses. However, as the conversation continued, I felt a little jealous of all the money I had missed out on. I have a great life, but I won't be cashing out and making tens or hundreds of millions of dollars.

Then, I found my thoughts drifting to The SOURCE. Almost immediately, my posture changed, a little smile came across my face, and I started thinking about what I had done. I started with an idea. It was an idea inspired by another local business leader: that employers could collaborate intentionally to create an organization that would help stabilize the lives of people who came to work for us, and become a "trusted and knowledgeable relationship" for our people in an ever-more-complex world. Twenty years later, more than twenty thousand people have had access to the services through twenty-eight member companies. It has been replicated in various forms across the entire United States. Oh, and I did not make a dime.

As I sat there listening to the stories, admiring the acumen and work that went into creating economic value in all those deals, I realized I could have spent my time doing that, too, and it would have been fun to talk about.

I found myself happy and at peace as I thought of all the economic value-creation in the lives of tens of thousands of people, because a few employers took a chance on an idea that they would not be able to denominate in cash. I even thought, "Give me all your money, or give me this, and I'll take this."

At a certain point, we start to define success differently. You get less satisfied with just making more money. Put another way, you start becoming less motivated by what other people value and more by what you value. What inspires me is that the people I have helped have gone on and done amazing things.

From a broader perspective, this is also a way to see and create more value in capitalism as a system. At its core, capitalism is the ability to build systems that add value. So, you come up with a new, more efficient idea, and you can deliver some product or service better, faster, cheaper, whatever it is. But at the same time, you are increasing the well-being of everyone involved in that value-creation chain, from your suppliers to people who work for you to customers. And I think the unfortunate thing is the current form of practiced capitalism is just extractive—extractive in dollars. Every time a value-creation event gets monetized, that value is extracted from the business in terms of money.

The prevailing social contract is: you come to work for me, and I will pay you this and give you benefits. I don't owe you anything else; what you owe me is a good day's work. It's about a good day's work for a good day's pay. There is no sense of responsibility for the well-being of those individuals outside of that. It's up to them to figure out what to do with that money. It's not my problem. But we've seen that this, and the system's complexity, have left many people behind. They don't know how to navigate the system well or take advantage of opportunities.

Yet we have an opportunity to measure value-creation in different ways than just cash, and to say, I'm not going to be extractive running my business. No, I'm not saying what my professors would have said: that profit is wrong and everybody should make the same amount of money because they all have value. I think you can make a fair profit, and you can, you know; and so can people who are degreed professionals and hard workers. There's plenty of money to be had doing this.

The other kinds of value are substantial and lasting and can't be taken away. I mean, when you start talking about the type of value that Liza Alvarez, whom I speak about in the last chapter, acquired, and the impact she's had across her life, and the influence she's had on family members and colleagues, the ripple effect of that value is significant, but you could never extract it in dollars. It's much more significant. And the opportunity to run a business in a way that drives value in a community and for the people that work for it is a great honor. You couldn't write me a hundred-million-lion check and make me happier.

CHAPTER SEVENTEEN
THE INTEGRATION

Earlier in this book, I shared my journey of disintegration—compartmentalizing different aspects of my personality. I did this because I have found a profound parallel between my journey and our collective experiences as business leaders, where we, too, tend to compartmentalize different aspects of ourselves.

But re-integration is possible. I have found it personally and professionally, and they go together. We have at our fingertips the best possible tools to create the more positive outcomes we want to see in our world. However, we have yet to be taught how to use those tools effectively. We have been conditioned to think that using those tools is somehow "weak" or "bad business."

Many people scoff at "triple-bottom-line" thinking because it is easy to measure money. So, when all value is denominated in cash, it is understandable that the result becomes a very disintegrated system.

Here's a small example: Let's say I have figured out a straightforward way to make a widget so I can sell a premium widget at a great price and deliver it in five days instead of the standard thirty days. I sell my widgets for one hundred units per widget.

It costs me only twenty units to make that widget. The easy math is that I make eighty units a widget! Customers like my widget because it eliminates the lead time, meets all their specs, and is reliable (an "easy button"), so they are willing to pay one hundred units per widget for all this. Now, it so happens I have a patented process for making my widgets the way I do, and it takes special training for someone to run the process to make those widgets.

What other value is created in this system that differs from the 80-unit "profit?" The value of the activity and the people who participate in and benefit from the activity do not get measured. The most obvious answer is the technical training to teach someone how to run the process. Assuming this skill is adaptable to other areas of life (work or personal), imparting that knowledge to a person or team of people increases their value to themselves, us as employers, and the community at large.

In addition, I have to pay a premium for technical talent, which adds economic value to the individuals who learn how to run my process, which is good for them and their families. My quick illustration is that we do this sort of training *all* the time in our enterprises. We also teach people how to use their health insurance, their 401ks, their HSAs, how to navigate our employee assistance programs, and so on.

We are constantly teaching people. And we're not just teaching the mechanics of a job. It's like parenting. We are role models for many things. So, we have a strong competency in teaching by nature. We are teaching how to run a meeting, negotiate with a vendor or a customer, have difficult conversations, plan an event or celebration, and manage a project. We teach values and practices such as being on time, being prepared for meetings, investigating root causes of problems, working efficiently, asking the next question, understanding customers' needs, and general problem-solving skills. And all that is before I get into any of the specialties covered by the vast array of enterprises we can run.

Put another way, I am not arguing that we need to make a 180-degree or 30-degree change in behavior. With some intention, what we need to do would take perhaps a five-degree change.

Here is another perspective. At one point, I was conversing with one of my coaches, and I was frustrated about how I was unable to "get through" to a particular person in my life. My coach first asked me to recount a recent conversation, which I gladly did with great passion, in the hope of getting her approval of how well I handled it. She paused and said, "If this was your daughter, would you have handled it the same way?"

My first thought was, well, of course not. She is a teenager. She wouldn't understand. How is that relevant? Her point was that I would have used a different tool if it had been my daughter. I would have started with a different tone. I would have started by teaching and discussing discovery, and I would have had a lot more patience!

So, I had the tools. I didn't think (or want) to use them for this situation. Well, guess what? I returned, used the tools I would have used with my daughter, and came out with a very different (and much more positive) outcome. Now, I have a great relationship with my daughter, but the point is that picking someone I respect and love and have a deep desire to see be successful allowed me to realize I could use those tools with others.

Why would I not bring my best self to all my relationships? Well, because I have learned how to compartmentalize. I have become comfortable with being disintegrated. As I contemplate how to be more integrated and how to bring my best self to every relationship, I get better at using a better set of tools and have more positive outcomes. One example is substituting impatience with curiosity and "waiting until I can make my case" while wondering how someone else got to the conclusion they did.

The power of applying this idea to our workplaces and talent is that we can get beyond simple re-integration and get to what is being called "regeneration," which is returning *more* value than is being extracted.

Now, let's go back to our previous example of the widget. When calculated beyond the profit, the total value-creation in the system is the contribution to the human capital in the equation, and the ripple effect of that value beyond the individual.

This is our opportunity. We can complain about the complexities of running a business, the work ethic of certain generations, the regulations, the changing technologies, blah, blah. However, we still and always will need to work with and through the efforts of people to accomplish whatever we are attempting to achieve. The relationship is an incredible opportunity to create a regenerative system for people. All it takes is being intentional, applying the same principles of integration we use in our personal lives to our enterprises, and then practicing.

CHAPTER EIGHTEEN
HOW SYSTEMS THINKING CAN HELP US CREATE BETTER TALENT FLOW

"The definition of insanity," Albert Einstein is famously thought to have said, "is doing the same thing over and over and expecting a different result." As the writer Christina Sterbenz has pointed out, insanity might be repeatedly crediting that quote to Einstein—because he never said it. A fictional character in a book by the mystery novelist Rita Mae Brown did.[23]

But the point remains a good one. It's simply mad to keep doing the same thing and expecting a different outcome. Yet many of us have been doing this regarding talent: complaining about shortages, not changing how talent is cultivated, and hoping and wishing it would improve. If I didn't know better, I would think, as business leaders, we saw ourselves as victims!

---

[23] Christina Sterbenz, "12 Famous Quotes That Always Get Misattributed," *Business Insider*, October 7, 2013. https://www.businessinsider.com/misattributed-quotes-2013-10

I remember when this point first hit me. I was at a board meeting of an organization engaged in a capital campaign. Over lunch, the executive director previewed a beautiful video their team had developed. It told a compelling story of the need for this organization's services, including clothing and furniture for impoverished people. They had also been sharing the video with donors and found it effective.

In short, everything seemed great. It was a great organization. They offered excellent services in our community. They had great communication. They had a great team. And they had great support from donors.

There was just one problem: They needed help connecting with the people who needed these services. Somebody called it "our dirty little secret." They could reach donors more effectively than they could reach the clients they intended to serve. The clients were difficult to reach since they often did not access traditional media outlets. They also learned about community services mainly through word of mouth.

That's when, suddenly, it hit me: the people they were trying to reach were the kind of people who worked for *me*. I realized they probably needed this service, or their families or neighbors did.

They might not have considered responding to an ad from this nonprofit organization because there wasn't a pre-existing trusting relationship between them. But they knew, worked, and trusted me. I could tell one hundred people the next day. If I did, they could get the clothing and furniture they needed, which could only help them be more reliable employees and benefit the organization.

So, I did. It was easy. I just put a flyer in their payroll envelope. That was it. It simply outlined the services offered and the hours they were open. Many people took advantage, and they also spread the word to others.

Putting a simple message in pay envelopes about a beneficial service was a foundational step in helping establish the stability of our team (as I wrote about in my first book, *The Source*). However, the principle also applies to the next step, which is the focus of this book: investing in our employees to cultivate the talent we need now and in the future.

We need to see ourselves as the developers, cultivators, or curators of the talent our communities need in the future. This is the shift. This is the imperative. This is the opportunity to add real and lasting value. As employers, we can take responsibility for education and progression. It is how we change the outcomes.

It's a system-thinking principle popularized by one of my heroes, Peter Senge, a systems scientist at the forefront of organizational learning since publishing his classic text, *The Fifth Discipline: The Art and Practice of the Learning Organization*. It was also one of my first insights into the significance of systems thinking as an aid in helping us as business leaders tackle talent challenges—and choosing an alternative beyond our somewhat mad approach to date.

As Senge has pointed out, people often misunderstand the term "systems thinking" because the word "system" tends to make people think of computer systems or some kind of amorphous system that we can blame for things turning out the way they do.

He is trying to help people understand how an organization can function more effectively, since we all live in "webs of interdependence." He suggests that the simplest way to envision this is to think about your existence in a family. A family is the most close-knit system. You can see and probably name most of the players. However, there remains a complexity of interactions among all the members of that system, and there are inevitable outcomes from those interactions that no one intended.

The same is true in an organization—as you undoubtedly have experienced! So, what then is systems thinking, and how does it help? It's about moving from seeing individual parts to whole systems, from linear cause and effect to interlinkages or circles of causality, from static snapshots to processes of change over time, and from visible solutions closest to us to actual systemic changes that create leverage.

Put another way, systems thinking is a discipline that integrates the core learning disciplines of:

- Personal mastery, which is about "continually clarifying and deepening our personal vision, of focusing our energies, of developing patience, and of seeing reality objectively."
- Mental models, which are "deeply ingrained assumptions, generalizations, or even pictures of images that influence how we understand the world and how we take action."
- Building shared vision, which is "the practice of unearthing shared pictures of the future that foster genuine commitment and enrollment rather than compliance."
- Team learning, which starts with dialogue, "the capacity of members of a team to suspend assumptions and enter into genuine 'thinking together.'"

While the "thinking" aspect of all of this might make you suspect it is merely academic, Senge explains that the point of understanding system thinking is a highly pragmatic one. In his words, it is "to understand how it is that the problems that are most vexing and difficult and intransigent come about, and to give us some perspective on those problems [to] give us some leverage and insight as to what we might do differently."[24]

While this book is not intended to offer a deep dive into systems thinking, I do want to go a little further to whet your appetite, because it has had such a powerful influence on me and my thinking about talent systems—and because it invites us to see the critical connections between pressing social problems and our workplaces. It also encourages us to ask the all-important questions: What can we do in our own house? What behaviors can we change that will impact the outcome—regardless of whether anyone else changes anything? This is where we move out of "victim" territory. If the current "system" does not provide us with the talent levels we need, what if we take action to ensure we have the talent levels we need in the future?

Easy? *No!* But *possible?* Yep!

To see how this applies to the talent challenge before us, let us first consider the laws of systems thinking:

How the 11 Laws of Systems Thinking Can Help Us Rethink Talent Systems

1. Today's problems come from yesterday's "solutions."

Peter Senge tells the story of a rug merchant who saw a large bump in the center of one of his carpets. He stepped on it to flatten it out. But then he saw another bump appear in another

---

[24] Peter Senge, "Introduction to Systems Thinking," from the IBM series "Leadership Lessons for a Smarter Planet," August 5, 2014. https://www.youtube.com/watch?v=eXdzKBWDraM

spot. Again, he stepped on it to flatten it out. And again, he saw a new bump elsewhere. Finally, he lifted a corner of the carpet and saw an angry snake slither out. It's a great example of this first law of systems thinking, which suggests that people may be confused about the true cause of a problem because it is simply shifted from one part of a system to another—with those who think they solved the problem in one part of the system never seeing that it is merely showing up elsewhere.

How can this help us understand and more effectively address problems in the talent system? Let's take a look at the facts.

- Before World War II, only 15 percent of high school students went on to higher education (most from upper-income families.)
- After World War II, college attendance soared, primarily due to the GI Bill. However, most Americans did not attend college because most jobs did not require it.
- In 1970, only 26 percent of middle-class workers had any education beyond high school.
- The 1970s also saw the shift from higher education for education's sake to a need for pre-professional studies and a translation to work after graduation. For many, being considered middle-class or getting a middle-class job requires a college degree.
- In 2013, 33.6 percent of 25- to 29-year-olds had a BA. More recently, as of 2017, according to the US Census Bureau, 33.4 percent of the adult US population had a bachelor's degree or higher education (up from 28 percent in 2006), with 20.8 percent holding bachelor's degrees. In 1940, when the US Census Bureau began collecting education data, only 4.6 percent of adults held bachelor's degrees.

- Now, nearly 60 percent of all jobs in the US economy require higher education—which means if you don't have a college degree, you are quickly pushed out of the middle class.

In 2014, *Washington Post* columnist Catherine Rampell wrote a bold piece titled "The college degree has become the new high school degree." It was based on a new report from Burning Glass, a labor market analytics company, that employers increasingly require a bachelor's degree for positions that once didn't—including the most basic, entry-level jobs.

Were college degrees actually required for these jobs? In many cases, they were not. However, many human resources departments have appeared to use them as a simple screening tool. As Rampell put it: "Bachelor's degrees are probably seen less as a gold star for those who have them than as a red flag for those who don't. If you couldn't be bothered to get a degree in this day and age, you must be lazy, unreliable, or dumb." There is little evidence to support such a sweeping generalization.

However, the system responded because we put "four-year degree" in our job descriptions, and more young people acquired four-year degrees. Then, suddenly, we had more college-educated people unable to find a job that required a college degree. Worse than that, we had many more young people unnecessarily burdened by significant debt, which led to a ramifying set of consequences—including many millennials and Gen-Zs finding a home purchase out of reach financially. And this, in turn, has a depressing effect on job growth and the economy. What's more, we have had qualified people without college degrees turned down for jobs that didn't require them—plus a shortage of people with needed technical skills they might have acquired at a trade school. In short, today's problems come from yesterday's "solutions."

So, what is the lesson learned?

We need to take a more holistic look at the talent system. We must rethink how we get kids into the workforce faster after high school and create an ongoing link between work and education. We could explore, for example, creating more of a balance between work and school, through which it would take longer to graduate, but the individual could end up with a job in a field they were genuinely interested in—and no debt. This would be far less punishing for kids who are not sure what they want to do. It would allow them to test their interests and make small education and vocation changes over, say, a six-year timeframe.

Consider, for example, establishing internships in partnership with local high schools. If we want to change behavior in a system, why not focus on how we can do that tomorrow? It's easy to walk into a high school down the street, introduce yourself, and start a conversation. We can't wait for schools and colleges to figure out how to prepare young people for the changing world of work. It will be too late! We must get involved in the conversation and offer to participate in the solution.

There is much more to this, of course. But the point is that instead of continuing to step on the rug and having problems pop up elsewhere, we need to look at talent as a system and examine—and own—our role in it.

2. The harder you push, the harder the system pushes back.

Have you ever seen a business respond to a decline in demand for a once-successful product by pushing for more aggressive marketing, perhaps combined with reducing the price? It seems like a tried-and-true strategy.

However, many have found that an increase in marketing costs and a decrease in price lead to a decline in revenue. And then what happens? The business has to start cutting expenses somewhere to compensate—and guess what? Cutting expenses can lead to a decline in quality. And guess what happens then? You guessed it. The company begins to lose even more customers.

This is an example of the second law of systems thinking that Senge describes as "compensating feedback." We see this happen at all levels of systems—from the individual to the family to the community to organizations to the government. The harder you push, the harder the system pushes back.

What about in terms of talent? Consider job training and upskilling efforts. The more money the system gets, the more training hours are completed, but those hours are not making our workforce more robust. These programs work for a while. Billions of federal dollars flow through our state workforce development systems and are paid to contractors who administer job training and then report back results to renew the contracts. The performance success metrics for these programs are abysmal. However, because classes are often free for job seekers or offered to employers for "free," they are often well-subscribed. So, we measured the number of hours of training or the number of people trained, and we thought it was successful.

Then we do it again and ask for more money. Large companies that make their money are awarded these government contracts. However, the data suggest that we have yet to significantly move the needle on the number of skilled people in our workforce over the last fifty years. Job-training contractors only have to track clients, placements, and metrics for thirty to ninety days, but does that change the lives of people the system is intended to help over the long haul? There is precious little evidence of that.

Our system relies on various government grants to put people through short-term training. However, individuals who need help are often not given a robust set of tools to help them continue to grow functionally in the talent system over the long haul.

For two decades, I have been a staunch advocate of employers working together to help stabilize the people who work for them, rather than relying on government funding. But the second law of systems thinking suggests that this overlooks the fact that the harder you push, the harder the system—in terms of government funding—pushes back. So, considering compensating feedback, what if we recognized that there is ample opportunity for employers to play differently in this system?

Instead of doing more of the same, we need to figure out how to deploy that funding differently within the system. What would change if we could get funding to build a lane where education and work could happen for people simultaneously, and employers were incentivized to participate when they created pathways with timelines—"graduating" from one position to another? We need to ask these questions to apply the principles of systems thinking to create a more effective talent system.

3. Behavior grows better before it grows worse.

There was once a *New Yorker* cartoon in which a man sitting in an armchair pushes away a row of dominoes that looked like they would fall on him. Then he relaxes, feeling he no longer has to worry. Problem solved. Meanwhile, the dominoes fall in a semi-circle behind him and eventually fall on him with greater force than they would have initially.

Senge shares this story as an example of the third rule of systems thinking: behavior grows better before it grows worse. Or, as he explains: "Low-leverage interventions would be much less alluring if it were not for the fact that many work, *in the short term*." (Emphasis added.)

We see this at play in the talent system through what I call the habit of getting people into "Job #1," and that's it. We spend so much money and effort getting people into a first job, which looks great to funders. But when those placements do not make a person more robust in the talent market, we inevitably continue to fund efforts to push under-skilled individuals around from one relatively low-skill job to another. In the short term, it looks like an improvement. Ultimately, we have a bigger problem, because no one has looked beyond the first domino. (To be fair, these are people and not numbers, so as this happens throughout their lives, they become cynical and disaffected toward their employers and jobs.) The lesson: We will not solve our talent issues if we don't look at the whole system.

4. The easy way out usually leads back in.

"We all find comfort applying familiar solutions to problems, sticking to what we know best," Senge writes. It's known, he adds, as the "what we need here is a bigger hammer syndrome." It also doesn't work because if that familiar solution were easy—and effective—it would be working already!

Yet, this is precisely what we do in response to talent challenges. In the wake of the COVID pandemic, employers nationwide have faced massive talent shortages. In fact, as of late

2021, more than one out of two companies globally reported facing talent shortages—more than triple over the past decade.

And this is unlikely to end anytime soon. By 2030, Deloitte projects that there will be 2.1 million unfilled jobs in manufacturing alone.

Why is this happening? There are many reasons. Older employees are retiring, and there needs to be more skilled talent to fill the void. COVID also changed how people relate to work. They want more, and they are less willing to compromise. And there are other reasons, no doubt including some we likely don't yet understand.

Now, consider how we, as employers, have responded to this shortage.

Increasing wages has been the most common—and familiar, "easy"—response. Amazon, Bank of America, and Chipotle have done it. McDonald's increased their wages by a whopping ten percent. Target increased its hourly wage to twenty-four dollars an hour. According to the federal Bureau of Labor Statistics, nearly two-thirds of payroll workers in the US private sector saw wage increases in the second quarter of 2021 that were 5 percent or more higher than in the second quarter of 2020.

This has been the equivalent of pushing "the easy button": offer more money and benefits. The problem is, it's not fixing the talent system. Nor, in non-pandemic times, has raising wages given us a more robust and flexible workforce.

What if we consider a more systemic solution rather than the familiar, easy, ineffective one? For example, what if we, as employers, started doing something different—something bold and smarter?

What if we start changing our expectations of ourselves regarding talent development, planning, and "owning" education? Education, after all, is the single most important ingredient in getting the talent we need. As Senge observes, sometimes the true solutions are obvious. But very often, they are off in the darkness.

5. The cure can be worse than the disease.

Have you ever known anyone with a drinking or drug problem and wondered, "How did that happen?" When they took their first drink or hit, there is very little likelihood that they did it thinking they would develop a problematic dependency that could make their life worse. On the contrary, they likely tried it and discovered it helped ease some burden they were carrying. Perhaps stress. Perhaps uncomfortable shyness around people. Perhaps the pain of a past trauma. Or maybe the burden of a mental illness, such as depression.

Research shows that countless people who have developed a dependency on alcohol or drugs have done so in the process of self-medicating—that is, trying to "cure" some problem they were dealing with. Then, over time, the dependency grew—and, as Senge puts it in this fifth law of systems thinking, the cure became worse than the disease. The original stress, shyness, trauma, or depression became ever more complicated by the adverse effects that inevitably come with an alcohol or drug dependency.

This principle holds true not only in the case of alcohol and drugs but also in many aspects of life—including, yes, the talent system. While Senge does not explicitly address talent systems, he does make the point clear through a discussion of what he describes as "ill-conceived government interventions [that] are not just ineffective, they are 'addictive' in the sense of fostering increased dependency and lessened abilities of...people to solve their problems."

Sound familiar? In response to COVID, the federal government directed *trillions of dollars* in spending, tax cuts, loans, grants, and subsidies to Americans. Trillions. It's hard to conceive of just how much money that is, but David Schwartz, author of the children's books *How Much is a Million, If You Made a Million,* and *Millions to Measure,* has thought a lot about it and puts it this way, to emphasize just how vast the difference between a million and a trillion dollars is. He says if you counted a million seconds, it would add up to eleven and a half days. If you counted a billion seconds? Thirty-two years. So, what about a trillion seconds? Thirty-two *thousand*—that is, 32,000 years.

What happens when this much money is distributed to people and organizations? That's a complicated question, of course. But this is clear: it does not magically fix all our problems. On the contrary, in the case of our talent challenges, it has, in certain ways, indisputably made the problems worse— by giving people the opportunity to depend on free government income instead of working. Chances are we all know someone who did the math: "I will earn only two dollars more per hour by working than not working. It's not worth it—because, comparatively, going to work would mean earning the equivalent of only two dollars an hour." For countless employers dealing with the repercussions of this well-intentioned but shortsighted response, the cure has been worse than the disease! And it is hardly a once-and-done dynamic.

"The phenomenon of short-term improvements leading to long-term dependency is so common," Senge writes, "it has its own name among systems thinkers—it's called 'Shifting the

Burden to the Intervenor.'" That is, it shifts the burden to the entity trying to help. According to Senge, the result is that it leaves "the system fundamentally weaker than before and more in need of further help."

A true cure requires the engagement of all key players in the system, including employers, educators, government, and employees. Indeed, for employers who get this, and do this work, and network with others who get it, and build vibrant talent networks utilizing enlightened education suppliers, there will be a new reality in talent selection. For the others, it will be a tough environment to survive in. The same goes for education providers.

6. Faster is slower.

"For most American business people," Senge writes, "the best growth rate is fast, faster, fastest. Yet, virtually all natural systems, from ecosystems to animals to organizations, have intrinsically optimal growth rates. The optimal rate is far less than the fastest possible growth." He goes on: "When growth becomes excessive—as it does in cancer—the system itself will seek to compensate by slowing down, perhaps putting the organization's survival at risk in the process."

Allow me to put this a little more personally. As a hobby, I drive race cars. I was driving a car on a track recently as my instructor stood on the track, watching. He radioed me as I approached a turn, cautioning me to slow down.

"If you want to get around the track, you have to slow down going into a turn so you can speed up coming out of it," he said. "Power won't fix this problem." In other words, "fast, faster, fastest" is not always the way to go when you want to achieve the best results.

Even when facing big nagging problems, such as in talent systems today, it behooves us to remember how complex the system is and not act quickly based on a partial assessment of the problem and a rush to a potential solution.

Optimal solutions require intentionality and planning. We need to consider what our talent wants and what it will do for us in the future, not just the present. To be effective beyond our immediate needs as employers, we also must be intentional about where we want our talent to go over time. This is about being enterprise-centric and talent-centric.

And, before you let yourself off the hook, imagining you don't have the time to learn how to think like this, consider this: we think this way all the time in our businesses regarding capital planning, sales planning, product life cycles, and more. Why not with talent? Seriously, why don't we apply this level of rigor to the way we develop talent?

Indeed, the reality that larger companies are doing this already makes it all the more imperative for small to mid-market companies to do it. The Amazons and the Googles of the world have hundreds of people on teams thinking through this issue. If we don't do it as well, these large companies will design the future the rest of us will have to adapt to. They will also be in a much better position to compete for talent, leaving small and medium-sized businesses far behind. I know I don't want that; if you're reading this book, I doubt you do. The good news is that we don't need to.

7. Cause and effect are not closely related in time and space.

If you've ever spent a day on the water and forgot to put sunscreen on, only to return home and find yourself nursing a nasty sunburn that evening, you had a good, simple, clear example of cause and effect. The cause: being out in the sun without sunscreen. The effect: sunburn. This is such a simple example that some elementary school teachers use it to demonstrate the principle of cause and effect to children. Or they might point to a student holding a big heavy pile of books that falls to the ground. Or a child holding onto an ice cream cone for too long on a hot summer day.

These examples suggest that cause and effect are closely related in time and space. However, in any complex system, such as the businesses we run, cause and effect are not closely related in time and space, and our failure to understand this leads to many additional problems and false solutions.

The same is true regarding the talent system and the learning that needs to be at the heart of developing it. It is true about learning in general. For example, I am currently working on learning how to play the piano. At fifty-seven years old, I did not expect to take one lesson and play one of my favorite Billy Joel songs after being shown the music to it. Learning is a journey. But I do expect that, with diligence, I will be able to play that song at a pace that someone will be able to sing. Learning is a long game.

So is talent development—with cause and effect not closely related in time and space. We need to invest time, effort, and money in identifying our current and future needs and what it will take to meet them, to have the results not just today but in five, ten, and twenty years from now.

I hope you will see, as I do, that all of this should make talent development attractive to us as prospective employers. If we can win this game, it will take others years to catch up. It will become a competitive advantage for talent acquisition and customer acquisition and retention.

Here's what I mean: If you do well at this, and can attract better talent that can adapt quickly to fast-changing circumstances, and can problem-solve at the speed of the market, it can help make your business and your talent more stable. You will also attract and retain customers who appreciate (and will pay for) a greater level of organizational agility.

As a manufacturer, more of our biggest business customers are increasingly concerned about the culture of their suppliers. You may have experienced this, too, as more big-scaled, branded companies are looking for suppliers with a story around social responsibility or civic engagement. Even Walmart, which succeeds by delivering low prices, is expecting more of its vendors in these ways. So are Starbucks, Patagonia, and Apple.

Developing talent is not only a good story. It will help you better serve the evolving needs of your customers. Maybe not today. Cause and effect are not closely related in time and space. But the sooner you start, the sooner you win—and the better positioned you are to have a competitive advantage over those who fail to apply systems thinking to talent.

8. Small changes can produce big results—but the areas of highest leverage are often the least obvious.

"Tackling a difficult problem is often a matter of seeing where the high leverage lies, a change which—with a minimum of effort—would lead to lasting, significant improvement," Senge writes. "The only problem is that high leverage changes are usually highly non-obvious to most participants in the system," he continues, adding: this is what makes life interesting.

Systems theorist Donella Meadows described leverage as "a small shift in one thing that can produce big changes in everything." Others have likened leverage points to acupuncture points—"places where a finely tuned, strategic intervention is capable of creating lasting change, creating positive ripple effects that spread far and wide."[25] Senge uses Buckminster Fuller's illustration of the trim tab on a ship. "It is only a fraction the size of the rudder. Its function is to make it easier to turn the rudder, which, then, makes it easier to turn the ship."

I love this principle! It is the beauty of calling all employers to the table! *Leverage*. It is at the heart of the reason I wanted to write this book. Each one of us can impact the system by investing in talent development. Even if we only have a few people working for us. Small changes *everywhere* will have a tremendous impact. Most of our enterprises are "small." So, if we start with our businesses and work on building our networks in our communities, there will be a significant shift over time.

I have another example. Think of the fulcrum and lever. If the fulcrum is in the right place, it can move the world. Or think about the fulcrum on a teeter-totter. It is more effective in the middle than at one of the ends.

Now imagine a three-way teeter-totter that involves the government, education systems, *and businesses* trying to solve our talent problems. Until now, we've only had two sectors trying to solve the problem: the government and education systems. I suggest we have not effectively solved it because one of the three key players has been left out. *Us!*

---

[25] Brooks, Rod. "How We Could Achieve Equity - Wendy Brooks & Partners." *Wendy Brooks & Partners*, 26 Jan. 2023, www.wendybrooks.com.au/2023/01/26/how-we-could-achieve-equity/. Accessed 3 Dec. 2024.

We, as employers, stand at one of those intersections where a little effort can generate a huge amount of change. We are the only sector at the intersection of wage earning and need. We are a key leverage point that can enrich the talent system in ways that serve our current and future needs. This applies to our companies' current and future needs. It also applies to the needs of the people who come to work for us—including their wages, education, and career development. We also must consider our community's current need for employment, and future needs for people who are better educated and have more relevant technical skills.

"There are no simple rules for finding high-leverage changes, but there are ways of thinking that make it more likely," Senge writes. "Learning to see underlying 'structures' rather than 'events' is a starting point.... Thinking in terms of processes of change rather than 'snapshots.' is another."

And once you learn to see this way, you can't "unsee" it—nor forget that we occupy a key, as-yet-overlooked leverage point in the talent system.

9. You can have your cake and eat it, too—but not all at once.

Many apparent dilemmas, such as...happy, committed employees versus competitive labor costs...are by-products of static thinking," Senge writes. "They only appear as rigid either-or choices because we think of what is possible at a fixed point in time." Real leverage, he adds, lies in seeing how both can improve over time.

I believe this is at the root of the talent system's problem. As employers, we have been historically selfish. If we invest in training and development, we want to keep that talent. This way of thinking is highly problematic.

It reminds me of a cartoon I saw years ago that may have been inspired by Henry Ford. In it, the CFO asks the CEO, "What if we train them and they leave?" and the CEO replies, "What if we don't train them and they stay?"

We run dynamic, ever-changing businesses. If we contribute skilled talent to the system, the system will supply skilled talent to us. As the Disney song from *Frozen* goes, we must "Let it Go." Again, this is a long game, but these are the thought paradigms we need to shift.

If we start educating in our organizations for our employees' next jobs, if we take on some responsibility and make some investment—if we all do that collectively—we raise the net talent in the system, which will help all of us. In short, we can have our cake and eat it, too—just not all at once.

10. Dividing an elephant in half does not produce two small elephants.

This may be one of the most straightforward laws of systems thinking to grasp. As Senge writes, if you divide an elephant in half, you don't have two small elephants. You have a mess. Systems have their integrity. "Their character depends on the whole."

He adds: "The current system is perfectly designed to give you the results you have." The reality is that very few, if any, of us are happy with the current system outcomes. The problem is we only "see" our enterprise. We do not see it in the context of a larger system.

As people responsible for enterprises, this may be the most challenging piece for us to see. It is hard to predict or "see" all the skills someone coming to work for us has, or how they acquired them. The same can be said when they leave us for other opportunities. It is hard to predict how or where they will put what they have learned into practice. This is because we are most concerned about our enterprise and do not see our enterprises as part of a larger talent system. That is why, to succeed now and in the future, we need to be enterprise-centric and people-centric.

But if we could get there, how much more invigorating would it be to think about what possibilities we are preparing our talent for? If we educate our talent to meet current and future demands, we will divide education into super-relevant pieces.

11. There is no blame.

Senge's explanation of this law is so simple and concise that I will quote it here in its entirety:

> We tend to blame outside circumstances for our problems. "Someone else"—the competitors, the press, the changing mood of the marketplace, the government—did it to us. Systems thinking shows us that there is no outside; that you and the cause of your problems are part of a single system. The Cure lies in your relationship with your "enemy," which is very like ourselves.

I have been in so many meetings over the years in which I find that employers are very quick to blame talent problems on others. They say: "People are lazy. They don't want to come to work." Or, "Look at what schools are turning out these days. I hired a high school kid. He doesn't know anything."

What is so surprising for me is that we are business leaders who clearly got into business because we could solve some kind of problem no one else was solving, or we could do it better. We are problem-solvers! But we don't think like problem-solvers regarding our talent.

The blame game never solves problems. Only a "no blame" attitude will. One of my favorite stories that illustrates this point is about Ruth Jones-Hairston, who spent thirty years as an educator in the Grand Rapids Public school system.

As a principal, she was nationally known for improving student outcomes and parent engagement—and many sought her counsel. As a leader, she recognized that the mission of her school was to educate students. But she also recognized that some of those kids were showing up hungry, often dirty, and with no shoes or inadequate shoes.

So, she started holding her teachers and staff accountable with what she called "the grandchild perspective." If this were your grandchild, she would ask, what would you do? And she took action: she installed washing machines and dryers. She connected with local nonprofits to provide clothes. She also reached out to community donors to provide breakfasts.

Some teachers rebelled. They said, it's not my job to ensure they are fed and dressed properly. And she said, you're right, it's not. Our job is to educate. But all these things they bring to school hinder us from doing our job. So, we will fix the barriers so we can do our job. Don't blame anybody. Just fix it.

I say we take a page from the late Ruth Jones-Hairston's book—and as employers, leaders, and problem-solvers, we stop blaming others for our talent problems. As soon as we point the finger, we abdicate our ability to solve this problem for our enterprises. We're acting like victims.

Instead, let's just fix the damn barriers. Together, we can drive change faster than any other sector in the country. So, let's get to work!

CHAPTER NINETEEN
DRAGONS AT THE THRESHOLD

Beekeeping has become popular in recent years, largely in response to reports that there has been a 60 percent decline in beehive populations since the late 1940s, or what scientists call Colony Collapse Disorder. This first brought attention to beekeeping as a hobby, and from there, people learned that they could help by having small hives in their backyards or on their rooftops. Suddenly, hives seemed to start popping up everywhere.

I joined the bandwagon a few years ago—but, honestly, not because I was primarily motivated by saving the bees. I thought my daughter might be interested (she wasn't) and that it would be an opportunity to enjoy "hyper-local" honey and overcome my fear of bees. This fear stems from the fact that I'm horribly allergic. If I'm stung, I break out in hives (no pun intended) and get highly itchy and feverish.

And while it thankfully has not happened to me, I know that I could go into anaphylactic shock within as soon as five minutes, which can cause loss of consciousness, shock, or other symptoms that can be fatal.

One day, I was moving the hive with Carrie, my executive assistant, when I accidentally dropped one corner, and the bees came out. Carrie saw them and stood still. I saw them and ran. Guess who they followed? Me. They swarmed all around my eyes, nose, and face.

I later learned that bees can detect fear pheromones in humans or other animals. And when they detect it, they emit a pheromone of their own to the rest of the hive that says: Threat! That's why they chased me as I ran madly across the yard and left calm Carrie alone.

Ah, fear. Whether we know it or not, it influences us so much. Extensive research studies have shown that fear decreases risk-taking.[26] And bold new ideas, such as what I am discussing in this book, tend to trigger a fear response, at least in many people. That's why Malcolm Gladwell's work on how change happens has been so significant to innovation and business.

In *The Tipping Point: How Little Things Can Make a Big Difference*, Gladwell identifies categories or stages of how new ideas spread—or what he calls the diffusion of innovations.

First come the Innovators, who represent about 2.5 percent. They are willing to take risks and, as the name suggests, develop new ways of doing things.

Then comes the Early Adopters, representing about 13.5 percent of the population. Early adopters are thought leaders

---

[26] S. Wake, J. Wormwood, and A.B. Satpute, "The Influence of Fear on Risk-Taking: A Meta-analysis," *Cognition and Emotion* (Vol. 34, 2020, Issue 6), pp. 1143–1159; published online March 2, 2020: https://www.tandfonline.com/doi/full/10.1080/02699931.2020.1731428

who know the need for change and are comfortable adopting new ideas.

Next comes the Early Majority, representing a hefty 34 percent of the population. A bit more cautious, these people want to see evidence that the innovation works before they are willing to adopt it. But they are eager to try something new before the rest of the population.

Fourth comes the Late Majority, another 34 percent of the population. These folks are skeptical of change and willing to consider doing something different only after most others have done so.

Finally, there are what Gladwell calls the Laggards. This not insignificant group represents about 16 percent of the population. They are generally wedded to the old ways of doing things and highly skeptical of changing them.

Which are you? If you are reading this book, you are in one of the first three categories. You're an Innovator, Early Adopter, or in the Early Majority. That's good news!

But, of course, you still need to reckon with the challenges and obstacles that come with a new way of thinking about talent. So, let's consider them in turn.

Fear

A 2001 Gallup News poll states Americans' greatest fear is of snakes. Fear, of course, is an emotion.

Now consider the facts. According to a more recent 2021 Centers for Disease Control study, 695,547 Americans die of heart disease a year, 605,213 of cancer, 416,893 of COVID-19, 224,935 of accidents, and 162,890 of stroke.

How many Americans die of snake bites a year? Approximately five. In fact, when was the last time you saw a snake that wasn't in captivity?

So, fear trumps logic every time. Of course, many people who run companies are courageous and innovative. But they also hear a lot of bad advice from others, including human-resources professionals and attorneys, who are hired to "manage risk."

They advise about all the things that could go wrong. They trigger fear in the minds of would-be actors who think, "Oh, crap, we don't want that problem." Leaders become motivated not to act and to simply maintain the status quo.

I should add that it's not the individual attorney or human-resource professional's fault. Risk management is built into the system, and they are expected to protect the enterprise from some of those fears.

But often, those perceived risks may have come from one or two bad experiences. It doesn't necessarily take into account all the other good experiences.

Still, none of this helps us get to the continuous improvement that W. Edwards Deming advocated—or that we know is needed to address our talent challenges better.

Consider a case in point: When I talk about wanting to share talent with other companies in my community—collaborating so that people have somewhere else to progress to, if there is no more room for advancement at my company—a common reaction I get goes something like this:

"What if everybody ups and leaves your company? You can't have everyone leaving and run a successful business."

To this, I respond: Why do you think they would leave? Do you think my workplace is so bad that everybody is just waiting for a chance to escape? I know many people don't love their jobs, but they don't rabidly hate them.

You have to watch out for knee-jerk, fear-based reactions. They don't allow time to think about things, and take them as truth without consideration. It could be you or others are just on automatic, like the person saying: I'm afraid of snakes!

Lack of Understanding

Leaving aside the fact that many people lack an accurate understanding of our challenges around talent because they do not think about talent as a system, several other mistaken assumptions contribute to a lack of understanding of this issue.

For example, some people look at those working for them in dead-end jobs and think—even if they won't say it aloud—people make stupid choices in life, and that's why they end up where they are.

As I wrote about extensively in my first book, *The Source*, the reality is that sometimes people make bad choices, and very often, people are thrust into circumstances that make life more difficult for them. Maybe they grew up in poverty or a crime-ridden neighborhood. Maybe their parents were unable to care for them properly. Maybe they had a terrible accident somewhere along the line. Or maybe, like Eric, the man I wrote about in Chapter Ten, they were caught between not having the skills they needed to get a better job, and being unable to leave their job to develop those skills because they had a family to support.

Another mistaken assumption is that we are all competing for the same talent. In reality, there are so many different needs and skill levels—and if anything, we don't have a great system of finding the people who are a good match for us instead of the employer up the street.

A third is cost. Some people reject the idea of cultivating, let alone collaborating, on talent because they think of it as an additional cost, while a more helpful way to think about it is as an investment, which could earn you more of a return.

Finally, here's one more. Many of us assume that people are only interested in their starting hourly wage—and perhaps think: How can I compete with local fast-food restaurants, which pay people seventeen dollars an hour plus education benefits? The reality, however, is that many people are looking for more than that. They are looking for a place to get on a journey to success. Perhaps where they can earn full health insurance and 401(k)s. A place where they feel respected and have a sense of purpose. So, why not design workplaces that speak to that, instead of getting sucked into reductive thinking that we're all competing based on who can offer the highest hourly wage?

Thinking It's a Lot of Work

Yes, we think it's a lot of work. And maybe it is! But like learning an instrument or any other worthwhile endeavor, a long-term horizon is useful. No one has to overhaul their talent system this week, any more than I can play Mozart, having only recently taken up the piano. But once again, the point is to take small steps toward continuous improvement.

Failure to Accept Leadership

One day, one of my managers asked an employee to come in early—four o'clock in the morning—to work extra hours. She had worked for us for ten years and readily obliged. But when she showed up in those wee morning hours, she realized she had forgotten to bring her employee badge, which functions as a key card. Security would not let her go in and required her to go home to get it. Then she got written up for being late.

I talked with my former human resources head about this, asking why didn't they just let her in.

We have a policy in place for a reason, she said.

Well, why not change it? I asked.

We can't change policies, she said.

I looked around over both my shoulders and then said to her, *I'm pretty sure we are "we."*

We are the leaders. We are the people who need to make changes.

I don't mean to suggest that making changes like the ones I'm talking about in this book is easy. I know from experience that they are not. I still feel frustrated that I have not yet been able to make as much progress in my company as I want to.

But it would be a far graver mistake to abide by the old, unworkable paradigm we operate under regarding talent. It could go back to my development. I spent much of my life unsure of what I wanted to do. I tried accounting, engineering, and other things. I also tried lots of ways to work around my dad. So, I am comfortable with iterating and problem-solving.

I am also OK with being a person on the leading edge, which people sometimes say is also the bleeding edge. I'm OK with that. If I can make a difference to just a handful of people and someone else can figure out how to bring this to scale, I'm OK with that too.

It may be a little corny, but I find inspiration in the famous starfish story by Loren Eiseley: [27]

Once upon a time, there was an old man who used to go to the ocean to do his writing. He had a habit of walking on the beach every morning before beginning work. Early one morning, he was walking along the shore after a big storm had passed, and he found the vast beach littered with starfish, as far as the eye could see, stretching in both directions.

Off in the distance, the old man noticed a small boy approaching. As the boy walked, he paused occasionally, and as he grew closer, the man could see that he was occasionally bending down to pick up an object and throw it into the sea. The boy came closer, and the man said, "Good morning! May I ask what you are doing?"

The young boy paused, looked up, and replied, "Throwing starfish into the ocean. The tide has washed them up onto the beach, and they can't return to the sea by themselves. When the sun gets high, they will die unless I throw them back into the water."

The old man replied, "But this beach must have thousands of starfish. I'm afraid you won't be able to make much of a difference."

The boy bent down, picked up yet another starfish, and threw it into the ocean as far as he could. Then he turned, smiled, and said, "It made a difference to that one!"

My ending to this story is that we (employers) have the opportunity to make sure none of the starfish end up on the beach to begin with.

---

[27] https://eventsforchange.files.wordpress.com/2011/06/starfish11.jpg

CHAPTER TWENTY
PLANTING SEEDS OF CHANGE

When I first met Liza Alvarez, I had only recently taken over the company from my father. I was young and inexperienced, and I had my hands full trying not to bankrupt the company. At nineteen, she was even younger, had barely finished high school, and had her hands full as the single mom of a one-year-old.

Today, she is the president of Bodega San Marcos in Grand Rapids, Michigan, working on an PHD EdD in organization development, and is a role model for her thirty-plus nieces and nephews—as well as countless others, who have crossed her path in workplaces from Butterball Farms to Vi-Chem, a Grand Rapids-based resin pellet company, to Bodega San Marcos.

What enabled her to succeed and give back to so many others, despite coming from a family where neither education nor career had been valued? I caught up with her recently to ask what support in the workplace had to do with it.

Her story is super-inspirational because, as I told her, the difference between us is that I didn't come out of a family that struggled. I was surrounded by examples of people who attended college and enjoyed success. She didn't have that, but she is an excellent example of continuous employment and education.

She is also a great example of how change happens: one person at a time. When people come to work for us, as employers we stand at the intersection of need and income. We don't understand all their needs, but we do have influence in that intersection. What we choose to do with that influence is a game-changer. Being intentional about it is a great opportunity. We can't always control what that influence will do, but we can be intentional about it.

Put another way, she is an example of what happens when leaders see investment in people (talent) in an open-handed and community-minded way. Each of the three employers she worked for—Butterball Farms, Vi-Chem, and Bodega San Marcos—believes in investing in their talent and removing barriers, especially the cost and scheduling barriers of obtaining ongoing education. Now, Liza has impacted people in her roles within these businesses and inspired many people in her family and countless others in our community. Her story is a great example of a value-multiplier that does not *get picked up* (show up?) on the cash-denominated scale of modern capitalism.

Here's what she had to say.

I come from a traditional Hispanic family, even though I am a third-generation American, in that graduating from school is not important. My mother didn't work much outside the home and was a single mother of eight children. She didn't finish school, and we lived off welfare. Many of my aunts, uncles, and cousins were in the same situation.

And having kids right away is just what you do. So, Alex, my oldest, was born when I was a senior in high school, and my mom didn't say, "Well, you need to go back and finish school." It was just something in me that said I wanted to do this. And so I took the bus to school with a newborn child just to finish high school. Alex was born in December, and I finished school in May of the following year.

I barely graduated, but then I needed a job. I had a child to raise. My godmother knew people at Butterball Farms who said it was worth working there. She talked with Sarah, the HR person at the time, and got me an interview, and I started working probably a couple of days later.

It was my first real job. I worked in operations at night. It wasn't easy because I was a single mother working nights, plus the requirements of working sometimes six or seven days a week and long hours. Then, I learned about an opportunity as a receptionist, and I moved into that for a time. I thought an office job as a receptionist was a big deal.

That's when I met you [Mark Peters], and you were the first CEO I had ever met. You were busy just taking over the company, but I knew you had a vision even back then. I remember your mission statement on the wall: "Enrich Lives." Those words impacted me as I could not comprehend a business owner interested in "enriching lives." It had nothing to do with the core business. I also remember those early conversations when The SOURCE was being thought of, and we were beginning to discuss issues like daycare. I also remember not having a car, and you sold me your Nissan Z for around five hundred dollars. It was pretty slick and fast. And, of course, having a kid in that car wasn't ideal. But you knew I was without a vehicle and things like that made a difference. You reached out and connected with people when you saw a need and a way you could help.

At one point, you also talked to me about going to college. This convinced me that I wanted to be an accountant because we needed one, and I was doing some accounts payable work from the reception desk.

You said, "You should attend school, and we'll pay for it." I started at Davenport College and did a semester, but then I realized I didn't want to be in accounting or go to school at that time. But it planted a seed for lifelong learning.

Meanwhile, financially, I realized I didn't get overtime as a receptionist. Plus, I had a passion for operations. And I learned that you can't get where you want to go by just, you know, letting it happen. You've got to work and make it happen. There are opportunities, but you have to be strategic about where you want to go and what you want to do. So I tried to see the big picture and said, Okay, where do I want to go? I later moved back to operations as a team lead.

Eventually, I had the highest-performing team. And I was doing things that I didn't realize impacted the company. But it satisfied me because I wanted to be the best, and I wanted to be successful. And I knew the bigger impact I could make, the higher I would go.

And then, I became pregnant again with my second child, Daniel, and stopped working for a time.

But working at Butterball was such a good experience. There, I started seeing, yeah, life can be different. And when I saw that, I wanted it.

After Daniel was born, I joined Vi-Chem, another organization around the corner from Butterball, with more opportunities to move up. When I started, I was again working nights in a quality control position for them. But they needed somebody in Human Resources. Back then, HR was a "personnel" position doing a lot of paper-pushing, and it was not a pretty job and not viewed in the best of light. Paychecks were wrong, and the organizational culture wasn't strategic, so people in HR were getting yelled at.

Vi-Chem needed someone bilingual in their HR, so they offered me the position. I didn't have any background, experience, or education, but what they needed was somebody who could communicate with people. At first, I thought I couldn't afford to take on an office job. I needed overtime. So, I initially turned it down, and they were okay with that. I mean, I wasn't their star candidate, either.

But something kept telling me, you should do this. The bigger opportunity was what it could lead to in the future, so I went back and said, You know what? I'm going to give it a shot.

I thought about it like this: I didn't have to be the HR example I had witnessed and experienced; I just didn't have to be that person. I'm going to make a difference, and I'm going to take the role seriously. I had a great HR mentor and was given opportunities to get involved in all aspects of the business, so I was involved in many different things. Those experiences helped me understand the business as a whole.

I was in my early thirties then, and Len [Slott, the CEO] said, if you go to college, I'll pay for it. So here again, somebody said if you go to college, I'll pay for it. And he was willing to bend to the tuition reimbursement rules and pay 100 percent. I took it a bit more seriously this time, and that's when my education started. At this point, I felt I could apply the business concepts to my experience and tie the conceptual with the actual, which felt meaningful. So, I got a knack for it and got my master's, which Vi-Chem paid for.

What was an amazing experience was when The SOURCE was launched, and Vi-Chem became part of it. That allowed me to get involved with others, network, talk about similar situations that we, as businesses, were having, and engage in outside-of-the-box thinking. It was unique to have people come together who could make things happen. It reminded me of your [Mark Peters] mission of "enriching lives." Still amazed that these business owners would come together to help people. It aligned with what we did in my family and communities, but I had never experienced or heard anything good from an agency, let alone an employer. I was curious and proud to be included. It wasn't my friends and I sitting around at dinner saying, oh, you know, wouldn't it be great if…? At The SOURCE, we had people around the table who could make things happen.

It offered me some critical guidance and networking. It was cutting edge to have all these different types of organizations come together so you can make quick decisions and say, yeah, we're just going to do this.

One example is the wellness program. Businesses weren't doing it, but we brought the right people around the table and just started making it happen. You had business leaders willing to invest, which was unique. I just don't think that you see that all the time. Usually, you work for one employer. But this was an employer group that worked together.

Then, I could bring things back to the Vi-Chem that I learned because we all had similar workforces, dealt with similar issues, and believed in helping and caring for people. So, I spent eighteen years working there.

Today, I'm working on my doctorate and am the president of Bodega San Marcos. Many people ask me, "Why are you getting your doctorate?" Part of it is about breaking history, generational curses and whatnot, and making a difference for the future.

I have a very large family. My mom was one of twelve kids, and I have seven nieces and nephews. All of my aunts and uncles had a lot of kids, so there are tons of cousins. Very few of us have college degrees, and only two have master's degrees. I'll be the first to have a doctorates degree.

I see a difference in the next generation in my family, what they're doing, and how they live. They're not just following the traditional path traditionally laid out for us. I think they take education and opportunities more seriously.

I have thirty-something nieces and nephews, and I'm pretty close with every single one. And so I would say—it's hard for me to talk about myself like this—but I would say the kids all look up to me and come to me when they have questions about anything—whether it's business or anything like that. So, I think it does make a difference.

It also makes a difference in the workplace and my community interactions. I have very good friends with whom I have been connected since my Butterball days. I was just given the opportunity to positively impact their lives through my work and on personal levels. I tried to pay forward what business owners like you [Mark Peters] and Len [Slott, CEO of Vi-Chem] had done for me.

I didn't have the money or the resources to care for people like those who helped me, but I've been put into positions and given stewardship over resources that allowed me to help. And I've had those business examples of leaders who invest in people and the community. And people don't forget that stuff. So I've been able to, in turn, make those impacts as well. And, yeah, it's good.

As the CEO of a company myself now, I also love the idea of supporting talent development—even if they go elsewhere. It's so important, as you've always said, Mark: talent development is not just for my business. That stuck with me.

I can think of many people I have worked with who have gone on, and you can see the impact that it's had on their lives. These are people who others might not have given a chance to realize their dreams or aspirations, however big or small they might be.

I've had so many managers come to me and say, "Oh my gosh, so and so is leaving." I'm like, "Well, you know, it's an opportunity. We can bring somebody in who will bring something different to the table." Maybe the other person has been there ten years, and we're not thinking differently anymore. We're not doing anything differently. And maybe a new set of eyes and way of thinking might have a better impact. Sometimes that doesn't happen, but the opportunity is there.

Plus, people will go elsewhere if I can't help them advance. So, my focus is helping them be successful, whatever that looks like. You can tie people into a contract after paying for their education, but that's not what I would do. I think you help people and you take care of people. There is nothing more rewarding than that. In my experience, people stay longer without a contract when taken care of.

But, you know, when you start getting the legalese and putting things in black and white, it's like, okay, it's just a little different, you know, naturally. It's typical, and I get it. I've been in HR and written many HR policies and things. But I had gotten away from doing much of that early on, tying people up. If they are happy and I can help them succeed wherever, that's great. The success positively impacts them as individuals, their families, and our communities; what more could I ask for as a business leader?

It's up to me to keep people challenged and engaged and ensure they are offered an environment where they feel valued, like they're contributing, and happy. It's not for everyone, so if it's not for them, they're probably not the right person for me.

People should be able to go where they want with no strings attached when, you know, we're offering that help and assistance, whether it's college education or just offering them an opportunity. Many people say, Yeah, we're going to invest in this person and get them trained, and then they're just going to leave. But if that is the case, it's not an individual issue. There may be a more significant issue going on in the organization.

Ultimately, that community is still better off when that person leaves if they got the education, and we're all still better off. If you look at it from a broader perspective, you will see that someone positively impacts another area. So, your web has spread. You're casting your net of influence further. These very examples and experiences provided opportunities for me and drove my success.

CONCLUSION

Early in this book, I acknowledged that a driving question of my life has been: can capitalism and compassion coexist? For those of you who have stuck with me to the end, it seems only right to share the answer I have come to.

Suppose you understand capitalism to be a system that is about extracting as much profit margin as possible from any set of activities, and you measure that profit in dollars. In that case, I don't believe capitalism and compassion can coexist.

But if you can think about capitalism as adding value, and you define that value as, yes, monetary but also in terms of human flourishing—the ability to gain skills that help you be a better parent, a better spouse, a better finance person, a better whatever it is you're pursuing, or you have always dreamt of pursuing, even if it means you leave the organization—then I do believe capitalism and compassion can coexist.

I do believe we have an opportunity as entrepreneurs to drive a lot more value into our people and our communities than we ever actually set out to do. We have the ability to have that influence and impact.

However, when we focus strictly on retention and protecting the enterprise, we are taking ourselves out of having an opportunity to be something much more vital. After all, if your mindset is protection, and you're living from a fear or scarcity mindset, you can't play an abundance game. You simply can't play a scarcity game and an abundance game simultaneously.

Focusing on retention is focusing on a symptom rather than the root problem. I want to emphasize again that I understand the impulse. I recently had someone in a critical position resign, and suddenly we were doing things today that we didn't have to think about yesterday. Everyone knows it's a lot of extra work when someone leaves.

That's why some people are resistant to this idea. They think, I don't want to go through this rehiring and retraining again and again and again. But the reality is you will anyway. At least *this* way, you can expect and plan for it.

After all, we have to be realistic that if you're a small company, you don't have a career path, especially for specialists. So, just embrace that fact. Don't be afraid to give them the most relevant training and education. You'll end up with a more resilient business.

What's more, at some level, if you have people who are working for you and can thrive or flourish, it is almost by default going to help your company succeed and thrive. I think it would be tough to have a group of thriving people come together and not do great work.

And here's the big takeaway: if you don't have some idea about bringing value to the people in your organization, and you don't see value in running an organization that frames value in terms of more than just profit, then you'll be in trouble. Ten years from now, companies that don't have this figured out just aren't going to get to play at all. They'll lose the war for talent.

When I set out to write this book, this deep sense of urgency drove me. The urgency was around what I see as those of us running small and mid-market companies regarding talent acquisition. I needed to "get the word out" to as many of my peers as possible and scare people into action.

However, as I went to work on this, I realized that we also have an opportunity that only a few people do: not large corporations, not private capital, and not government. That's because the speed to integration is faster for small and medium-sized enterprises than for private equity firms and big companies. It's also more challenging for them to take a people-centric approach. These are our natural advantages to seize.

Of course, pointing out the need for a paradigm shift—going from a retention mindset to an investment mindset—is easy. However, doing it requires changing long-held mindsets, not just your own but those of many people around you.

If you have ever tried the Majic Eye puzzles, you know how pleasing it is when you can see the hidden image. Once you understand that all you have to do is shift the images a few frames by looking "past" the picture to see the "real" picture, they become fun and easy. But if you share them with someone who cannot see them, it can be very frustrating.

This is an excellent analogy for what I have attempted to do in this book. I want every employer to "see" the shift. To look past retention to investment. Why? Because we live in an amazing country with a vast population of individuals who seek significance and meaning. We also live in an amazing country full of businesses and entrepreneurs doing interesting things and solving challenging problems. We live in an amazing country with some of the best educational resources on the planet.

As employers acting in and dependent on the talent system, we are the only actors who can protect this amazing system we live in by tearing down the barriers to development, and understanding our role in this system. Understanding that our investment in the people who come to work for us is an investment in our future. Period. Regardless of whether or not that person continues to work in our enterprise.

So, if you are fortunate enough to have influence over an enterprise or organization that employs people, here is my challenge. Step back and look at all the people who walk in the door or log on daily to collect a paycheck and help you run your organization as they do. If you can, see them. See them as people with dreams and aspirations, people who have encountered fear and setbacks and hurt and failure, people who may be trading their dreams for a paycheck.

You stand in the unique position to open doors of development for those people, to show them a pathway to progress toward their goals. Just do it. Build a workplace that celebrates people who want to make change personally.

RESOURCES

i-3 Leadership

Apprentix: A platform for all businesses to start and run apprenticeships, and build phenomenal talent.

Butterball Farms, Inc. A quality butter and flavor solutions supplier to America's major brands that is dedicated to enriching lives—that is, being an agent of change for our employees, local community, and customers.

Dave's Killer Bread: An American brand of organic whole-grain products. The company is also well known for "Second Chance Employment," an initiative which increases employment opportunities for people who have criminal backgrounds.

Greyston: A nonprofit organization dedicated to providing employment opportunities and support services to individuals facing barriers to employment, such as homelessness, poverty, or prior incarceration.

Homeboy Industries: The largest gang rehabilitation and re-entry program in the world.

Managing the Future of Work: A Harvard Business School's project that pursues research that business and policy leaders can put into action to navigate the changing nature of work.

Manpower Group: The leading global workforce solutions company.

R.I.S.E. Up Program: A partnership between West Michigan Works!, Trinity Health in Grand Rapids, and The SOURCE, a nonprofit employee support organization. The program uses a seven-step career pathways process and aims to support entry-level employees to build career pathways into the healthcare industry.

The SOURCE: A network that brings together community, government, and private interests to leverage existing assets to strengthen the community's workforce.

US Chamber Foundation Talent Pipeline Management: provides employers and their education and workforce development partners with strategies and tools to co-design talent supply chains that connect learners and workers to jobs and career advancement opportunities.

ACKNOWLEDGMENTS

As the process of writing this book came to an end, I was filled with relief, wonder, and gratefulness. I felt relief because this was a four-year journey encompassing an entire manuscript rewrite, which occurred when my primary enterprise was going through a turnaround. I felt wonder because I was very pleased with the final product; sometimes, it is difficult to see the forest for the trees in a project like this. And I felt grateful for so many people's help, insight, time, and interest in the topic.

First and foremost, I want to thank Lisa Bennett, my ghostwriter. Her ability to listen, ask probing questions to get at the heart of my thoughts, and then put all those hours of calls into a format that both captured the ideas and my voice was absolutely amazing. She also kept me focused and engaged when I started to lose focus.

Second, I am grateful to my executive assistant, Carrie Link, whose enthusiasm for this work is undying and who kept us on pace—me in particular, which is no small task. In addition, she spent countless hours chasing down and scheduling interview candidates and podcast appearances and managing some of the social media content. She also first stumbled across the US Chamber of Commerce Foundation's Talent Pipeline Management curriculum, which widened the lens on the importance of the ideas in this book and the realization that large-scale work is already being done on talent pipelines and talent movement within large, scaled organizations.

Additionally, I would like to thank my executive team for their support of the ideas in this book, and their willingness to help me build a network of employers who are willing to consider building career opportunities across multiple companies that are not necessarily related.

I also want to thank all the people who took the time to contribute to the content of this book, including Liza Alvarez, CEO and partner of Bodega San Marcos; Peter Beard, senior vice president of Regional Workforce Development and UpSkill Houston with the Great Houston Partnership; Mike Brady, partner of Shelter Lab and former CEO of Greyston Bakery; Jamie Francis, Jason Tyszko, and Nikki DaSilva from the US Chamber of Commerce Foundation; Joe Fuller, co-leader of the Managing the Future of Work project and a professor at Harvard Business School; Geoffrey Jones, author of *Deeply Responsible Business* and a professor at Harvard Business School; Chris Layden, vice president and general manager of Global Industry Leader for the Manpower Group; Shana Lewis, vice president of Talent Acquisition and Workforce Development Programs at Trinity Health; and Andy Seth, CEO of Apprentix. Finally, I wish to thank a few people who have been mentors, fellow spirit leaders, and pioneers in investing in talent and doing real work to make real change in real people's lives every day: Fred Keller, chairman of the board at Cascade Engineering, and Deb Nankivell, CEO of the Fresno Stewardship Foundation.

ABOUT THE AUTHOR

Mark Peters is the chief executive officer of Butterball Farms, Inc., which was nationally recognized as one of The Best and Brightest Companies to Work For® from 2018 to 2024.

Long seen as one of the nation's leading C-suite visionaries, Mark has been recognized with the 2022 Lifetime Achievement Award by Vistage; the 2014 People 1st Award presented by McDonald's; and the 2008 Excellence in Urban Business Awards by Inner City 100.

Mark's company, Butterball Farms, Inc., is a second-generation family business based in Grand Rapids, Michigan. Butterball Farms is America's leading culinary butter and margarine producer and creates custom butter flavors for some of America's biggest brands.

His tenure at the company began at age twelve, on the floor of the factory—an experience that taught him firsthand about the challenges that frontline workers face. At the age of thirty, he took over the company, determined to lead a financially successful business that would also enrich the lives of its workers.

In 2003, Mark organized a pioneering group of CEOs and community leaders to found The SOURCE. This not-for-profit organization has helped thousands of workers navigate personal challenges interfering with their jobs, and delivered an average annual return on investment of 329 percent to its partner organizations. The SOURCE's west-Michigan-based model has been replicated in cities and regions in nearly ten states. Mark is expanding its mission to help frontline workers maintain their jobs and progress into better positions within or across partner companies.

Mark wrote about the model used by The SOURCE in his 2020 book, *The Source: Using the Power of Collaboration to Stabilize Your Workforce and Impact Your Community.*

Mark has appeared on podcasts ranging from Harvard Business School's pod, *Managing the Future of Work*, to the BBC News, the *Leadership Junkies* pod with Jeff Nischwitz and Craig Matthews, and his work and the work of The SOURCE have been the subject of features and profiles in numerous locales.

An engaging speaker and storyteller, Mark lives in Grand Rapids with his daughter and dog and is an avid sailor, biker, and skier.